ACTS

WESLEY BIBLE STUDIES

wesleyan
PUBLISHING HOUSE
wphstore.com
Indianapolis, Indiana

Copyright © 2014 by Wesleyan Publishing House
Published by Wesleyan Publishing House
Indianapolis, Indiana 46250
Printed in the United States of America
ISBN: 978-0-89827-882-8
ISBN (e-book): 978-0-89827-883-5

CONTENTS

INTRODUCTION

Carry the Torch and Pass It On

_____

Usually between eight thousand and fourteen thousand runners, chosen by organizers and sponsors of the Olympic Games, enjoy the privilege and responsibility of carrying the Olympic torch. For a few glorious minutes before passing the torch to the next runner, each torchbearer holds it high and runs a designated course. Crowds line the route and cheer on each runner. Although celebrities often carry the Olympic torch, anyone at least fourteen years old is eligible, as long as he or she is able to run a minimum of 437 yards. The Olympic Stadium explodes with thunderous cheers when the final runner enters, ascends a flight of stairs, and ignites the cauldron that emits a brilliant flame that burns until the Olympic Games conclude.

The inspired book of Acts, often referred to as the Acts of the Holy Spirit, gives us the feeling that we are witnessing an Olympic torch-bearing event. We read about heroes of the faith who carried the gospel torch along a divine route—from Jerusalem to Judea to Samaria and throughout their known world. As they ran the race set before them, they lit the way for lost souls to know the risen Savior.

PREPARING TO CARRY THE TORCH

After rising from the grave, Jesus taught His apostles for forty days and then instructed them to remain in Jerusalem for the baptism of the Holy Spirit. Only then would they be ready to take the gospel and carry it as His witnesses.

THE FIRST TORCHBEARERS

The apostles, particularly Peter and John, were the first to hold the light of the gospel high for all to see. On the day of Pentecost, three thousand Jews saw the light and believed. But the apostles experienced persecution at the hands of those who preferred darkness to light. Yet the light penetrated the darkness and many unbelievers in Jerusalem repented and trusted in the risen Savior. The book of Acts shows Peter carrying the torch as far as Caesarea, to the home of Cornelius, a Roman centurion.

THE TORCH PASSED TO STEPHEN AND PHILIP

Two Spirit-filled men, Stephen and Philip, who were chosen to care for the needs of the widows of Grecian Jews, became outstanding torchbearers. Stephen held the torch high as he addressed the Sanhedrin, and he experienced martyrdom for doing so. Philip ran with the torch all the way to Samaria and Gaza, where the Lord saved many lost souls.

BARNABAS AND PAUL SHARED THE PRIVILEGE OF CARRYING THE TORCH

Barnabas, a kindhearted member of the church at Jerusalem, became a torchbearer along with the apostle Paul, a former vicious persecutor of believers. Apparently, Barnabas had "seen the light" on the day of Pentecost and had become a model member of the Jerusalem church. On the road to Damascus, Paul had been blinded by light that emanated from the risen Son of God. He turned in faith to the Son of God and soon began to carry the gospel torch.

For a while, both men "ran" side by side as they carried the light of the gospel, but eventually they parted ways. The second half of Acts focuses mainly on Paul's missionary travels. The route he followed with the gospel torch in hand was long and difficult. He encountered many hardships, but he persevered. At the end of the race, he passed the torch to younger men like Timothy and Titus, but he rejoiced that God had given him the privilege of carrying the light to darkened souls. He testified, "I have finished the race, I have kept the faith" (2 Tim. 4:7).

Let this study of Acts inspire you to carry the gospel torch to the end of the race. And be sure to pass the torch to others.

CARRYING ON JESUS' MISSION

Acts 1:1–11

God wants us to carry on the mission Jesus began.

A preacher told a story about a group of boys gathered at a corner lot for a game of baseball. They chose teams and were ready to start the game, but when they took stock of their equipment, they discovered no one had brought a ball. Several kids had brought baseball bats, and nearly everyone had brought a glove, but no one had brought a baseball. "What are we going to do?" one boy asked. Another answered, "Let's just forget the ball and get on with the game."

Of course, a baseball is essential to a baseball game. Similarly, as this study points out, the Holy Spirit is essential to evangelism.

COMMENTARY

This passage forms a bridge between the gospel of Luke and the record of the Spirit's work through the early church. It looks back to the life and ministry of Jesus and sets the stage for the church carrying His ministry to the ends of the world. In Acts 1:8, Jesus marked out His plan for the flow of church history and the continuation of His ministry. Tradition tells us Luke wrote both the gospel of Luke and the Acts of the Holy Spirit through the apostles and the church.

He followed Jesus' promise and commission in Acts 1:8 as an outline for this book. The disciples waited in Jerusalem and received the Holy Spirit on the day of Pentecost (Acts 1–2). The church ministered and grew in Jerusalem (Acts 3–7). The church took the gospel to Judea and Samaria as they ran from the persecution that began immediately following Stephen's martyrdom (Acts 8–12). The last section of Acts gives attention to Paul's missionary journeys that started spreading the gospel "to the ends of the earth" (Acts 13–28).

The book of Acts probably was written around A.D. 63. This date seems best, because there is no reference in the book to four significant events that followed this time: (1) the result of Paul's imprisonment and trial; (2) the vicious persecution led by Emperor Nero in 64–68; (3) Paul's death in 66–67; (4) the destruction of Jerusalem and the temple in 70.

Forty Days with Jesus (Acts 1:1–5)

In my former book, Theophilus (the gospel of Luke, see Luke 1:1–4), **I wrote about all that Jesus began to do and to teach until the day he was taken up to heaven** (Acts 1:1–2; see Luke 24:36–53). Luke planned to complete in this second book what he had begun in his gospel. Here he would describe how the church continued to carry out Jesus' ministry. Both books were written after careful research (Luke 1:3) and personal experience (Acts 16:10–17; 20:5–6; 21:1–18; 27:1—28:16).

WORDS FROM WESLEY

Acts 1:1

The former treatise—In that important season, which reached from the resurrection of Christ to His ascension, *the former treatise* ends, and this begins: this describing the Acts of the Holy Ghost (by the Apostles), as that does the acts of Jesus Christ. (ENNT)

After His suffering and death, Jesus was raised from the grave just as He had promised (Luke 24:1–12). Then He showed himself to these men (Luke 24:13–36; Matt. 28:8–17; John 20:10–21:22). Jesus also gave many convincing proofs that He was alive, such as allowing them to touch Him and eating with them.

Jesus **appeared to them over a period of forty days** (Acts 1:3). This period of time is significant in the history of God's saving acts. It rained for forty days and forty nights after Noah entered the ark, and he waited forty days before exiting it (Gen. 7:4, 12, 17; 8:6). Moses stayed on Mount Sinai for forty days (Ex. 24:18; 34:28; Deut. 9). The twelve spies were in the Promised Land for forty days (Num. 13:25). Goliath challenged the Israelite army for forty days before David came and defeated him (1 Sam. 17:16). Elijah traveled for forty days to meet with the Lord (1 Kings 19:7–15). Jesus fasted and prayed for forty days as Satan tempted Him in the wilderness (Matt. 4:1–11; Mark 1:12–13; Luke 4:1–13).

WORDS FROM WESLEY

Acts 1:2

After having given commandment—In the third verse, St. Luke expresses in general terms, what Christ said to His apostles during those *forty days*. But in the [fourth] and following verses, he declares what He said on the day of His ascension. He had brought his former account down to that day. And from that day begins the Acts of the apostles. (ENNT)

During *this* period of forty days, Jesus spoke about the kingdom of God. This was a regular part of His teaching ministry before His crucifixion and resurrection. In his gospel, Luke used the word *kingdom* four ways. First, he used it to refer to a political realm or unit (Luke 4:5; 21:10). Second, he used it to talk about political or spiritual power and authority (Luke 1:33; 9:2; 11:17–18; 12:31; 22:29–30). Third, he used it to talk about the presence of God's reign in Jesus' ministry (Luke 9:27; 10:9, 11; 11:20; 13:18, 20; 16:16; 17:20–21). Fourth, he used it to describe God's coming dominion (Luke 11:2; 13:18, 28–29; 19:11–12, 15; 21:10, 31; 22:16, 18; 23:42).

Matthew presented the coming of God's kingdom as equal to His will being "done on earth as it is in heaven" (Matt. 6:10). He also indicated the disciples tended to view the kingdom as a political realm where they could hold positions of power (20:20–28). John 6:15 indicates this expectation of a political kingdom was found throughout the Jewish society. Jesus spent a great deal of time trying to convince His followers that His kingdom is not of this world (John 18:36).

On one occasion, while he was eating with them (proving He was not a ghost or hallucination), **he gave them this command: "Do not leave Jerusalem, but wait for the gift my Father promised, which you have heard me speak about. For John baptized with water, but in a few days you will be baptized with the Holy Spirit"** (Acts 1:4–5). These directions echoed Jesus' teachings about the Holy Spirit on the night before He died (John 14:15–30; 15:26–27; 16:5–16). They also remind us of John the Baptist's words about Jesus coming to baptize His people with the Holy Spirit (Matt. 3:11; Mark 1:8; Luke 3:16; John 1:33).

Focus on the Mission (Acts 1:6–8)

Jesus' promise that in a few days the disciples would be baptized with the Holy Spirit stirred their hearts and minds. **So when they met together, they asked him, "Lord, are you at this time going to restore the kingdom to Israel?"** (v. 6). Here again the disciples were looking for political realm. They longed for the end of all evil and the complete expression of God's royal authority. But Jesus still had another point of view.

He said to them: "It is not for you to know the times or dates the Father has set by his own authority" (v. 7). Times indicates chronological order. **Dates** or "seasons" (in some translations) carries the idea of the favorable moment. Jesus seemed to have been telling the disciples the chronology and the content of the future is beyond their knowing. The future is under the Father's authority alone.

Instead of worrying about when the kingdom would arrive, Jesus told them to focus on the mission He had for them: **You will receive power when the Holy Spirit comes on you** (v. 8). This promised power involves God's royal authority (kingdom) conquering Satan, the god of this age (2 Cor. 4:4). Luke tied this God-given power to the Holy Spirit (Luke 1:35; 4:14; Acts 10:38). Later the apostles preached with power (Acts 4:33). The power Jesus promised is the result of the Holy Spirit's presence in a community. Simply, rather than mere political position and prestige, Jesus gives the Holy Spirit and God's authority over the spiritual realm.

●

WORDS FROM WESLEY

Acts 1:8

But ye shall receive power—and shall be witnesses to me— That is, ye shall be impowered to witness my Gospel, both by your preaching and suffering. (ENNT)

God's power and authority can change anything. The Holy Spirit brings that power into our lives with His presence. The result and goal of a Spirit-filled community is that expression of God's power—in miraculous signs or soul-stirring messages—will call people to believe in Jesus as Lord and Savior. With the Spirit's powerful presence, Jesus' followers will be His **witnesses in Jerusalem, and in all Judea and Samaria, and to the ends of the earth** (1:8). This is their mission and the focus of their lives from now on.

The Ascension (Acts 1:9–11)

After he said this, he was taken up before their very eyes, and a cloud hid him from their sight (v. 9). Luke is the only New Testament author to record the ascension of Jesus (Luke 24:49–53). The phrase **taken up** or its equal appears four times in this chapter (Acts 1:2, 9, 11, 22). The word *up* shows symbolically that the ascension moved Jesus from the sphere of time and space, where He achieved our salvation. He returned to heaven to be with the Father. Paul implied this in Philippians when he said, "God exalted him to the highest place" (Phil. 2:9). The author of Hebrews also assumed Jesus left the physical world to reign "at the right hand of the Majesty in heaven" (Heb. 1:3). The cloud that hid Him from their sight may have been the cloud of God's glory (Ex. 40:34–35; 1 Kings 8:10–11; Matt. 17:1–8).

They were looking intently up into the sky as he was going, when suddenly two men dressed in white stood beside them (Acts 1:10). Angels are spoken of as **men dressed in white** (see Mark 16:5; John 20:10–12). **"Men of Galilee," they said, "why do you stand here looking into the sky?"** (Acts 1:11). Jesus said to stay in Jerusalem and wait for the Holy Spirit to come. When He issues a command to the angels in heaven, they obey immediately. It must have seemed strange to the angels for the apostles to stand staring up into the sky when Jesus had told them to stay in the city.

The angels not only prodded the disciples with a question, but they also delivered a promise about Jesus' return: **"This same Jesus, who has been taken from you into heaven, will come back in the same way you have seen him go into heaven** (v. 11). Jesus described His second coming this way, too: "They will see the Son of Man coming in a cloud with power and great glory" (Luke 21:27). The prophet Daniel foretold of "one like a son of man, coming with the clouds of heaven. He approached the Ancient of Days and was led into his presence. He was given authority, glory and sovereign power; all peoples, nations and men of every language worshiped him. His dominion is an ever-lasting dominion that will not pass away, and his kingdom is one that will never be destroyed" (Dan. 7:13–14). No wonder the disciples "worshiped him and returned to Jerusalem with great joy" (Luke 24:52).

WORDS FROM WESLEY

Acts 1:11

We freely own that Christ is to be adored in the Lord's Supper; but that the elements are to be adored, we deny. If Christ is not corporally present in the host, they grant their adoration to be idol-atry. (*Coster. Enchir.*, c. 8, n. 10.) And that He is not corporally present anywhere but in heaven, we are taught, Acts 1:11, 3:21, whither He went, and where He is to continue till His second com-ing to judgment. (WJW, vol. 10, 121)

The ascension inspires our minds and spirits with four decisive details. First, Jesus left this physical world to take His rightful place on the throne of heaven. Second, Jesus did not leave us alone in this hostile environment; the Holy Spirit came at Pente-cost. Third, the ascension brought Jesus' earthly ministry to a glo-rious and victorious close and began His heavenly ministry of intercession at God's right hand (Rom. 8:33; Heb. 7:25). Finally, as surely as Jesus left this world, He will return in power and glory (Matt. 24:30).

DISCUSSION

Don't you get weary of political wrangling and wars? Do you long for the return of Jesus? The disciples must have longed for a better world with Jesus in charge. They hoped He would restore the kingdom to Israel right away.

1. What do you want this study of Acts to accomplish in your life? Why?

2. Read Acts 1:1. "Theophilus" means lover of God. Do you think Luke wrote Acts to an individual named Theophilus? Why or why not?

3. Read Acts 1:3. What do you think "the kingdom of God" refers to? Why?

4. Read Acts 1:4. Why do you agree or disagree that we will not eat when we have our resurrection bodies?

5. What might have happened if the apostles had not waited for the Holy Spirit's power?

6. Compare Acts 1:9 and Matthew 24:30. What connection, if any, do you see between the mention of "cloud" and "clouds"?

7. Compare Acts 1:8 and 11. Why should believers shun idleness while waiting for Jesus to return?

8. Why do you agree or disagree that it is essential to "be" Jesus' witnesses as well as to do witnessing?

PRAYER

Father, please fill us with Your Spirit and open up opportunities for us to help create disciples in Your name as Your Son commanded.

THE SPIRIT-FILLED COMMUNITY

Acts 2:1–6, 12–18, 37–47

God wants to fill us with His Spirit and empower us to
live together in Spirit-filled community.

A recording secretary gave the following report at a church's annual business meeting: "We didn't lose any members this year. We didn't gain any members. No one was converted. No one was baptized. We had thirty-one members at the beginning of the year. We didn't lose any members. Nor did we gain any members. Praise God, we are holding our own."

As this study points out, the church can be a dynamic force for God. Instead of "holding their own," the early Christians experienced dramatic growth on the day of Pentecost. Empowered by the Holy Spirit, they proclaimed the wonders of God, Peter preached, and three thousand believed, were baptized, and were added to the church.

COMMENTARY

Acts 2 details the fulfillment of Jesus' promise to give His disciples power when the Holy Spirit came upon them (Acts 1:8). The outpouring of the Holy Spirit on Pentecost was different from anything God's people had experienced before. It took in all the believers. Previously in Israel's history, the Spirit only worked through specific kings, priests, or prophets. He worked by coming on them as needed, but He never stayed. The Holy Spirit ushered in a new era on the day of Pentecost. Until Jesus comes again, the Spirit will indwell and empower all believers to proclaim God's message.

All Together in One Place (Acts 2:1–6)

Pentecost literally means fiftieth day. The day of Pentecost, then, referred to the day after the Sabbath of Passover week (Lev. 23:4–7, 15–16). Pentecost, one of three great annual feasts of Israel, was preceded by Passover (Lev. 23:4–8; Num. 28:16–25) and followed four months later by the Feast of Tabernacles (Lev. 23:33–43; Num. 29:12–38). Pentecost also was called the "Feast of Weeks," because it was celebrated seven weeks after Passover (Deut. 16:10); the "Feast of Harvest," because the firstfruits of the harvest were gathered then (Ex. 23:16); and the "day of the firstfruits" (Num. 28:26).

WORDS FROM WESLEY

Acts 2:3

And there appeared distinct tongues, as of fire—That is, small flames of fire. This is all which the phrase, *tongues of fire*, means in the language of the seventy. Yet it might intimate God's touching their tongues as it were (together with their hearts) with divine fire: His giving them such words as were active and penetrating, even as flaming fire. (ENNT)

When the day of Pentecost came, they were all together in one place (Acts 2:1). The individuals gathered in prayer were obeying Jesus' command (Acts 1:4, 13–14). As they prayed together, there were three physical manifestations of the Holy Spirit's arrival: They heard **a sound like the blowing of a violent wind** (2:2). The Hebrew and Greek words for *spirit* also mean wind. **They saw what seemed to be tongues of fire that separated and came to rest on each of them. All of them** (the twelve apostles and the other disciples, the men, and the women) **were filled with the Holy Spirit and began to speak in other tongues** or languages **as the Spirit enabled them** (vv. 3–4).

Others outside the prayer meeting heard these sounds. **Now there were staying in Jerusalem God-fearing Jews from every nation under heaven. When they heard this sound, a crowd came together in bewilderment, because each one heard them speaking in his own language** or tongue (vv. 5–6). The Spirit-filled men and women communicated God's glorious grace to these curious individuals across language barriers.

●

WORDS FROM WESLEY

Acts 2:4

And they began to speak with other tongues—The miracle was not in the ears of the hearers (as some have unaccountably supposed) but in the mouth of the speakers. And this family praising God together, with the tongues of all the world, was an earnest that the whole world should in due time praise God in their various tongues. *As the Spirit gave them utterance*—Moses, the type of the law, was of a slow tongue. But the Gospel speaks with a fiery and flaming one. (ENNT)

I Will Pour Out My Spirit on All People (Acts 2:12–18)

This universal gathering of God's chosen people brought Jews from as far west as Italy and as far east as modern Iran. When the curious crowd gathered, **Peter stood up with the Eleven** (v. 14) to explain what God was doing. Peter began by citing an Old Testament prophecy: **"This is what was spoken by the prophet Joel: 'In the last days, God says, I will pour out my Spirit on all people. Your sons and daughters will prophesy, your young men will see visions, your old men will dream dreams. Even on my servants, both men and women, I will pour out my Spirit in those days, and they will prophesy'"** (vv. 16–18).

After quoting Joel's prophecy, Peter drove home the heart of God's message: "Everyone who calls on the name of the Lord will be saved" (v. 21). The Jews knew the Lord was their only source of salvation. But Peter's next point was that the Lord had come in a man named Jesus. He reminded them of Jesus' miracles and that they had rejected Him. Peter pointed to Jesus' death on the cross and to His resurrection (vv. 22–24). Then he said Jesus was "exalted to the right hand of God, [where] he has received from the Father the promised Holy Spirit and has poured out what you now see and hear" (v. 33).

WORDS FROM WESLEY

Acts 2:17

Q. Do we not discourage visions and dreams too much, as if we condemned them *toto genere?*

A. We do not intend to do this. We neither discourage nor encourage them. We learn from Acts 2:17, &c., to expect something of this kind "in the last days." And we cannot deny that saving faith is often given in dreams or visions of the night; which faith we account neither better nor worse, than if it came by any other means. (WJW, vol. 8, 284)

The Spirit Is for All (Acts 2:37–41)

When the people heard this—that they had crucified their Messiah—**they were cut to the heart** (v. 37). The heart was the center of one's personality as well as his or her emotions. The heart brought together a person's mind, emotions, and will. In other words, Peter's message cut through all the faulty thoughts they had about Jesus. It pierced through their rebellious wills and smashed their self-righteous feelings of pride with true conviction.

Jesus promised that when the Spirit came He would "convict the world of guilt in regard to sin and righteousness and judgment" (John 16:8). The author of Hebrews also pointed out that "the word of God is living and active. Sharper than any double-edged sword, it penetrates even to dividing soul and spirit, joints and marrow; it judges the thoughts and attitudes of the heart" (Heb. 4:12). Peter's message could cut his hearers to the heart because it delivered God's word with the Spirit's convicting power.

They . . . said to Peter and the other apostles, "Brothers, what shall we do?" (Acts 2:37). Now that they understood who Jesus was and what they had done in killing Him, they needed to know how to make things right with God. Peter's response was a repetition of one many in the crowd had heard before: **Repent and be baptized** (v. 38). This was the same answer John the Baptist had given to seekers before Jesus began His ministry (Matt. 3:1–2). The theme of repenting was Jesus' first message when He began to preach (Matt. 4:17). Both John and Jesus' disciples baptized individuals who repented and confessed their sins (Matt. 3:6; John 4:1).

The word *repent* primarily means "to change one's mind." And yet that change of thinking must be followed by changed behavior. John the Baptist told those who came to him to "produce fruit in keeping with repentance" (Matt. 3:8). To repent is to make a 180-degree turn in thinking about Jesus, necessarily resulting in changed behavior.

Baptism had been part of the ceremony used when a Gentile converted to Judaism. However, when John came he called Jews to be baptized (Mark 1:4–5). Jesus had instructed the disciples to carry on that ministry as part of the Great Commission (Matt. 28:18–20).

Peter's call to repentance encompassed the entire crowd (**every one of you**) and set new parameters for baptism (**in the name of Jesus Christ for the forgiveness of your sins** [Acts 2:38]). Baptism itself does not produce the forgiveness of sins. It is an outward, physical act that corresponds to the inner, spiritual act of receiving God's mercy and grace. Both the baptism and the forgiveness are only effective in the name of Jesus Christ—in His power and authority.

When you repent and are baptized in the name of Jesus Christ **you will receive the gift of the Holy Spirit** (v. 38). The grammar of the original language indicates that the Holy Spirit himself is the gift and not some special ability for ministry. **The promise is for you and your children** (v. 39)—the Jews, God's chosen people. The promise of salvation and the Holy Spirit is also **for all who are far off** (v. 39)—the Gentiles (Eph. 2:11–21). The gift of the Holy Spirit is offered to all kinds of people, in all places, and at all times. The Spirit will be given to all who repent and receive God's gracious forgiveness.

With many other words Peter **warned them; and he pleaded with them, "Save yourselves from this corrupt generation"** (Acts 2:40). He wanted to persuade as many as possible to repent and receive the Holy Spirit. This attitude spread so completely through the church that the apostle Paul said, "I make myself a slave to everyone, to win as many as possible" (1 Cor. 9:19). As a result of Peter's passionate plea, many responded positively. **Those who accepted his message were baptized, and about three thousand were added to their number that day** (Acts 2:41).

The Spirit Is Evident in Changed Lives (Acts 2:42–47)

These new Christians were transformed. They had a new purpose in life. They devoted themselves to several activities that are still essential in the church. Their devotion to these activities drove them to constant and persevering dedication. This devotion produced both the feelings and the actions of commitment.

First, **they devoted themselves to the apostles' teaching** (v. 42). This teaching included all that Jesus had taught them (Matt. 28:20). It would have included explaining the Old Testament prophecies about the Messiah's suffering as Jesus had done with them (Luke 24:25–32, 44–49). **The apostles' teaching** (Acts 2:42) is preserved for us in the books of the New Testament. When we persistently study the Bible, we too are devoted to the apostles' teaching.

WORDS FROM WESLEY

Acts 2:42

Are there, under the Christian dispensation, any *means ordained* of God, as the usual channels of His grace? This question could never have been proposed in the apostolical church, unless by one who openly avowed himself to be a Heathen; the whole body of Christians being agreed, that Christ had ordained certain outward means, for conveying His grace into the souls of men. Their constant practice set this beyond all dispute; for so long as "all that believed were together, and had all things common" (Acts 2:44), "they continued steadfastly in the teaching of the Apostles, and in breaking of bread, and in prayers" (v. 42).

But in process of time, when "the love of many waxed cold," some began to mistake the *means* for the *end*, and to place religion rather in doing those outward works, than in a heart renewed after the image of God. They forgot that "the end of" every "commandment is love, out of a pure heart," with "faith unfeigned"; the loving the Lord their God with all their heart, and their neighbour as themselves; and the being purified from pride, anger, and evil desire, by a "faith of the operation of God." Others seemed to imagine that though religion did not principally consist in these outward means, yet there was something in them wherewith God was well pleased; something that would still make them acceptable in His sight, though they were not exact in the weightier matters of the law, in justice, mercy, and the love of God. (WJW, vol. 5, 185–186)

Next, they devoted themselves to **fellowship** (v. 42). We often associate this word with church dinners and Christian friends. However, it is richer than that. In classical Greek, this word was used to describe things owned in common by the citizens of a city. For example, a public park was the property of all the citizens.

They all shared a part in it. The park was their mutual concern. In the New Testament, it is translated "take part" or "participate in" (Matt. 23:30; 1 Cor. 10:16–17; 2 Pet. 1:4). It is used to explain the purpose of Jesus' incarnation—since humans have flesh and blood, Jesus had to become one of us (Heb. 2:14). It was an active sharing with those in need (Rom. 12:13; 2 Cor. 9:12–13). Fellowship carries the idea of Christians caring for each other and is a proof of our relationship with Jesus Christ (Phil. 2:1–4). Fellowship expressed itself in two notable ways. On the one hand, it generated daily meals where **they broke bread in their homes and ate together with glad and sincere hearts** (Acts 2:46). On the other hand, their devotion to the fellowship also produced extraordinarily generous stewardship. **All the believers were together and had everything in common** (v. 44). Their attitude toward material things was transformed by God's love. **Selling their possessions and goods, they gave to anyone as he had need** (v. 45). John Wesley wrote that this generosity "was a natural fruit of that love wherewith each member of the community loved every other as his own soul" (ENNT). This attitude of generosity and love continued to mark the early church (Acts 4:32–35).

Then, they devoted themselves to worshiping God. One feature of their worship was the breaking of bread or Communion (1 Cor. 10:16–17). In the early church, the Lord's Supper was celebrated as a part of a larger meal. This practice had its roots in the Passover meal, which involved more than blessing the cup and breaking the bread. Their worship involved public meeting because **every day they continued to meet together in the temple courts** (Acts 2:46).

An additional facet of their worship involved prayer. The resulting answers filled everyone **with awe, and many wonders and miraculous signs were done by the apostles** (v. 43). Their worship constrained them to continue praising God for these signs and answers.

●

WORDS FROM WESLEY

Acts 2:45

But here a question will naturally occur: "How came they to act thus, to have all things in common, seeing we do not read of any positive command to do this?" I answer, There needed no outward command: The command was written on their hearts. It naturally and necessarily resulted from the degree of love which they enjoyed. Observe! "They were of one heart, and of one soul": And not so much as one (so the words run) said (they could not, while their hearts so overflowed with love), "that any of the things which he possessed was his own." And wheresoever the same cause shall prevail, the same effect will naturally follow.

Here was the dawn of the proper gospel day. Here was a proper Christian church. It was now "the Sun of Righteousness" rose upon the earth, "with healing in his wings." He did now "save his people from their sins": He "healed all their sickness." He not only taught that religion which is the true "healing of the soul," but effectually planted it in the earth; filling the souls of all that believed in Him with *righteousness*—gratitude to God, and good-will to man; attended with a *peace* that surpassed all understanding, and with *joy* unspeakable and full of glory. (WJW, vol. 6, 256)

The final area of ministry the church of Jerusalem conducted was outreach. Their active love for people in- and outside the fellowship and God's miraculous answers to prayer helped them enjoy **the favor of all the people** (v. 47). As a result, **the Lord added to their number daily those who were being saved** (v. 47).

DISCUSSION

Do you ever feel outnumbered by unbelievers at work or school? Is the situation somewhat intimidating? The disciples at Jerusalem were greatly outnumbered, but they spoke courageously about their risen Lord.

1. Read Acts 2:1. Why do you agree or disagree that Christians need to spend time in the presence of other Christians?

2. How do you know the "tongues" mentioned in Acts 2:4 were actual languages? What purpose did the tongues serve?

3. Why do you agree or disagree that Peter was well-versed in Scripture?

4. Has anyone ridiculed you for declaring God's wonderful works? If so, how did you respond?

5. Read Romans 8:9. Why do you agree or disagree that the Holy Spirit dwells in every Christian?

6. Does the church need another Pentecost? Why or why not?

7. Do you think the sharing of possessions and goods was necessary? Why or why not?

8. How would you answer someone who said the early believers at Jerusalem were Communists?

PRAYER

Father, thank You for Your Spirit in our lives—for His gifts and for how He prompts us to live in love and generosity that reflects You.

WHAT WILL YOU DO WITH THE RISEN JESUS?

Acts 2:28–38

Jesus, who died and rose again, is able to
forgive our sins when we repent.

Al-Masjid, "Mosque of the Prophet," in Medina, Saudi Arabia, is the second holiest site of Islam. The Green Dome in the southeast corner of the mosque is where the tomb of Muhammad is located. Many Muslims who perform the required once-in-a-lifetime visit to Mecca visit the Green Dome tomb.

Unlike Muhammad's tomb, the tomb in which Jesus' body was laid to rest is empty. He arose triumphantly from the dead and is alive forever.

This study shows the resurrection was central to the apostles' preaching, and it should be central to our faith and witness. Our faith is anchored to a Savior who died for our sins and rose again.

COMMENTARY

Peter's Pentecost sermon centered on Jesus Christ and His resurrection. "The resurrection of Jesus of Nazareth accredited by God to you by miracles, wonders and signs" (Acts 2:22) had forever changed the course of history. The greatest of these signs was the impossibility for death to keep its hold on Him (2:24).

Peter addressed the mostly Jewish crowd with the words of their own prophet Joel (2:17–21). He then ascribed the fulfillment of this prophecy to the person of Jesus of Nazareth (2:22–24). He then looked to David for further evidence that Jesus is the Messiah (2:25–28).

In 2:28–38, Peter argued for the validity of David's prophecy. His message through the Holy Spirit convicted his listeners. They asked, "What shall we do?" (2:37). Today we are faced with the same question: What shall we do with the risen Jesus?

David's Prophecy (Acts 2:28–35)

Peter made two arguments for the validity of the events of Pentecost and for Jesus of Nazareth (2:22) being the Messiah — the first from Joel's prophecy (Joel 2:28–32) in Acts 2:17–21, and the second from David's prophecy (Ps. 16:8–11) in Acts 2:25–28. These prophecies affirmed the extraordinary nature of what was happening and provided the context for the predicament the listeners found themselves in — accomplices to the crucifixion of Christ.

WORDS FROM WESLEY

Acts 2:28

Thou hast made known to me the ways of life — That is, Thou hast raised me from the dead. *Thou will fill me with joy by thy countenance* — When I ascend to thy right-hand. (ENNT)

Peter's listeners were God-fearing Jews from every nation (2:5). They had respect for their patriarch David. Peter's quotation from David would have been well-received and readily understood. But knowing the possible response of his listeners to David's words "you will not abandon me to the grave, nor will you let your Holy One see decay" (2:27), Peter took time to explain its message.

Peter confidently affirmed that David had died and was buried. Not only could the listeners be certain of this truth, but the evidence was present: **his tomb is here to this day** (v. 29).

If David had been referring to himself when he declared he would not be abandoned to the grave or his body see decay (2:27), then his tomb would have contradicted his words. South of Jerusalem, near Siloam, David's tomb was visible to all. Just a few chapters later, in Acts 13:34–38, while the apostle Paul was in Pisidian Antioch, he made the same argument—that David had died, was buried, and his body decayed.

But David's words were spoken prophetically. He knew God had promised that a descendent in the Davidic line would be placed on his throne (2:30). David spoke of the resurrection of the Christ (Messiah).

A review of 2 Samuel 7:5–16 gives God's promise to David through the prophet Nathan. Here he was promised that his "house and kingdom will endure forever" (2 Sam. 7:16). Later, in Psalm 132, David again sang of the Lord's promise by oath that "One of your own descendants I will place on your throne" (Ps. 132:11). David had confidence in the promise of God that a Messiah would come after him, who would defeat the power of death and the grave and establish an eternal kingdom.

In this passage, Peter made a bold claim: **God has raised Jesus to life and we are all witnesses of the fact** (Acts 2:32). Notice in verse 31 the reference to **Christ** (Greek) or Messiah (Jewish); in verse 32, Peter declared this Messiah to be **Jesus** by virtue of His resurrection. David died and was buried, but Jesus the Christ was **raised . . . to life** (v. 32). This is what made Peter's message so important and provided the essential foundation for the church and kingdom that was to follow. Peter and the apostles, and likely some of those in his listening audience, were eyewitnesses of both great miracles and the resurrection.

Without the resurrection, all effort would be in vain. The message of the resurrection was central to Peter's message, and it is central to the message of the twenty-first-century church. We cannot relegate our resurrection message to Easter, but every

Lord's Day should be remembered as a resurrection day. Every day Christians must be reminded that their lives and walks are because of the risen Lord.

There is yet another difference between David and his prophecy and the life of Jesus. Jesus has been **exalted to the right hand of God** (v. 33). **David**, on the other hand, **did not ascend to heaven** (v. 34). David does not sit at the right hand of God, a place reserved by the king for those he intended to give the highest honor. So David was not the Messiah, but Jesus sits in this exalted position of power and majesty. He has been placed in the position where **enemies** would be **a footstool for** His **feet** (v. 35). The symbolism here alludes to ancient conquerors who would place their feet on the necks or heads of their conquered foes as a demonstration of power. Not only is Jesus' resurrection important to grasp, but His placement by God in the supreme position of power over His enemies is critical to the present and future victory the Christian experiences in Christ.

WORDS FROM WESLEY
Acts 2:34

Sit thou on my right-hand—In this and the following verse is an allusion to two ancient customs; one, to the highest honour that used to be paid to persons by placing them on the right-hand, as Solomon did Bathsheba, when sitting on his throne (1 Kings 2:19); and the other, to the custom of conquerors, who used to tread on the necks of their vanquished enemies, as a token of their entire victory and triumph over them. (ENNT)

The Assurance That Jesus Is Lord and Christ (Acts 2:36)

David's witness through prophecy and the eyewitness of the disciples allowed Peter to boldly proclaim, **"Let all Israel be assured of this: God has made this Jesus, whom you crucified,**

both Lord and Christ" (v. 36). Notice at least three important items in this short verse.

First, there is no doubt that **this Jesus** is the one referred to in prophecy. This is the person designated by God as the Messiah. The facts point to one conclusion, and all Israel can be assured of this. There can be no other.

Second, **God has made this Jesus . . . both Lord and Christ** (v. 36). Notice how carefully Peter interplayed the use of **God, Jesus, Lord**, and **Christ**. The explicit meaning is that Jesus, with the full affirmation of God himself, is both Lord Jehovah God and Christ the Messiah. This also was noted in Peter's quotation that from Joel in Acts 2:21 (quoting Joel 2:32). There is no difference here between the heavenly Father and the Son. This is an overt reference to the Trinitarian nature of the Godhead—Father, Son, and Holy Spirit—and further affirms the deity of Jesus.

Third, note the use of the phrase **whom you crucified** (Acts 2:36). These were strong words of indictment to the listening Jews. The accusation was direct: "you . . . put him to death by nailing him to the cross" (2:23). *You* crucified the Messiah, Jesus the Christ. The evidence is overwhelming: There was no question that Jesus was God's chosen, but then you crucified Him.

The further implication is that as Messiah, Jesus the Christ is also the deliverer. While under the oppression of the Romans, the Jews looked for a messiah, but they looked for a political messiah, one who would free them from civil oppression. Jesus the Christ brought deliverance, but a different kind—freedom from sin and its effects. Today many do not teach of Christ's deliverance, only that His crucifixion and resurrection covers or somehow reduces the penalty of our sin. We must consider what a deliverer accomplishes—Jesus as the author of our salvation, intends not only for our ultimate salvation, but for us to be brought fully into God's presence as holy men and women. He is the "author and perfecter of our faith" (Heb. 12:2) whose intention is to present us "without fault and with great joy" to God (Jude 24–25).

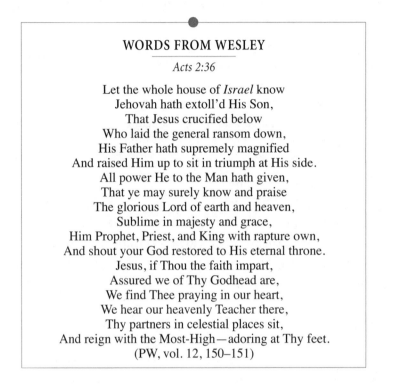

WORDS FROM WESLEY

Acts 2:36

Let the whole house of *Israel* know
Jehovah hath extoll'd His Son,
That Jesus crucified below
Who laid the general ransom down,
His Father hath supremely magnified
And raised Him up to sit in triumph at His side.
All power He to the Man hath given,
That ye may surely know and praise
The glorious Lord of earth and heaven,
Sublime in majesty and grace,
Him Prophet, Priest, and King with rapture own,
And shout your God restored to His eternal throne.
Jesus, if Thou the faith impart,
Assured we of Thy Godhead are,
We find Thee praying in our heart,
We hear our heavenly Teacher there,
Thy partners in celestial places sit,
And reign with the Most-High—adoring at Thy feet.
(PW, vol. 12, 150–151)

The Question (Acts 2:37)

What if someone approached you and said, "You killed the one person who could free you from death"? How would you feel? Such an accusation would cut deep, and remorse would set in quickly. Peter's listeners were stunned. When they heard Peter's sermon about Jesus Christ's death and resurrection, **they were cut to the heart** (v. 37). *We* crucified Jesus the Christ.

Certainly they felt sorrow and remorse for the gravity of their sin. Perhaps they were angry that they had become caught up with the hysteria of the crowd and fallen to the pressure. They were likely guilty, overcome with a feeling of deep anguish about their wrong actions. Each of these emotional responses can be imagined today, and we should experience similar emotions when each of us discovers that our individual sins nailed Jesus to the cross.

Now the crowd, full of remorse, addressed the apostles as **brothers**. No longer were these speakers opponents, but now one spiritual beggar asking another spiritual beggar where to find food. **"What shall we do?"** (v. 37).

The people weren't cut to the heart by the eloquence of the rough fisherman Peter who had preached a wonderful sermon. Rather, the presence of the Holy Spirit in the message of Peter and working in the hearts of the listeners brought about this heart-wrenching response.

The preacher cannot arouse the guilty conscience, nor can the preacher compel men and women to respond to the leading of the Holy Spirit. The preacher's job is to clearly present the truth of the Bible. The Holy Spirit is the one who makes it sink in, who enables it to cut to the heart. Do you listen to the Holy Spirit and let His message cut to the heart in your life?

The Response (Acts 2:38)

Peter's reply was most convincing—there is still hope. Despite the terrible state of our sinfulness, there is still hope. He said, **"Repent and be baptized"** (v. 38). Peter's message was not new. It was the message John the Baptist had brought: "The kingdom of God is near. Repent and believe the good news!" (Mark 1:15). And it was the message Jesus had preached: "Repent, for the kingdom of heaven is near" (Matt. 4:17).

Repent—turn your heart and mind away from sin and its enticements and replace it with a life with Christ. True repentance always leads to a change in the way you live.

One of the early actions Peter recommended is baptism. Salvation is based in the person of Jesus Christ, but the ready identification with Him in baptism seems to have been closely coupled with repentance in the New Testament. Baptism was an outward sign of what had happened within a person. As such, it was the natural next step for the new Christian. The call to **repent and be baptized** was extended to **every one of you** (Acts 2:38). There is no ethnic, gender, or age discrimination present in this call. Peter's hearers were diverse, yet none were omitted. The same salvation prophesied by Joel and preached by Peter is offered today: "Everyone who calls on the name of the Lord will be saved" (2:21).

Peter offered repentance and baptism **in the name of Jesus Christ for the forgiveness of** their **sins** (v. 38). The "name that is above every name" (Phil. 2:9), the name of Jesus of Nazareth, Christ the Messiah, offers the only sufficiency for the sin problem of the heart. He alone, through His death and resurrection, is able to provide forgiveness for sins.

WORDS FROM WESLEY

Acts 2:38

Repent—And hereby return to God: *Be baptized*—Believing *in the name of Jesus*—And ye shall receive the gift of the Holy Ghost—See the three-one God clearly proved. See ch. 26:20. *The gift of the Holy Ghost* does not mean in this place, the power of speaking with tongues. For the promise of this was not given *to all that were afar off*, in distant ages and nations. But rather the constant fruits of faith, even righteousness, and peace, and joy in the Holy Ghost. *Whomsoever the Lord our God shall call*— (Whether they are Jews or Gentiles) By His word and by His Spirit: and who are not disobedient to the heavenly calling. But it is observable St. Peter did not yet understand the very words he spoke. (ENNT)

But an additional ingredient is now available with repentance and water baptism: **you will receive the gift of the Holy Spirit**

(Acts 2:38). The Holy Spirit himself is the gift. Peter affirmed what John the Baptist had taught: "I baptize you with water, but he will baptize you with the Holy Spirit" (Mark 1:8).

Peter's reply to the question "What shall we do?" (Acts 2:37) is as applicable today as it was two thousand years ago. Repentance, baptism, and the gift of the Holy Spirit is for men and women today. What will you do with the risen Jesus?

DISCUSSION

Easter comes only once a year, but should the message of Easter resonate in our minds and hearts every day? What religion can point to its founder's empty tomb? Christianity rests on both an old rugged cross and an empty tomb. Our Savior is risen!

1. How is your faith impacted by the fact that Jesus fulfilled prophecy by rising from the grave?

2. Why are you looking forward to Jesus' eternal kingdom?

3. Read Acts 2:29–36. What differences between David and Jesus do you find in this passage?

4. Read 2 Samuel 7:16. How does this verse help you cope with news of international terrorism and war?

5. Why do you agree or disagree that the prophecy quoted in Acts 2:34–35 has both a present and future fulfillment?

6. Read Acts 2:36. How does your life reflect the fact that Jesus is Lord?

7. Do you agree that conviction of sin, as evidenced in verse 37, is infrequent in our modern culture? Why or why not?

8. Read Acts 2:38. How has repentance played a significant role in your life?

9. Why do you agree or disagree that baptism is not necessary for the forgiveness of sins?

PRAYER

Father, thank You for sending Your Son to die and rise again that we might be transformed more into Your image. May our lives reflect both deep repentance and a sense of Your powerful grace.

ORDINARY PEOPLE, EXTRAORDINARY GOD

Acts 4:1–20

Ordinary people become extraordinary witnesses
when they know Jesus.

Many countries greatly restrict the practice of Christianity. Morocco, for example, forbids people from distributing Christian books and pamphlets and does not allow Christian missionaries. Christians may be left alone if they do not try to share their faith, but it is strictly against the law to lead people to Christ.

Can you picture what it must be like to live in a land that does not allow Christians to evangelize? On one hand is the law of the land. On the other hand is the Great Commission. Would you obey the law or the Great Commission? This study answers this thorny question.

COMMENTARY

The context of Acts 4 is closely related to that of Acts 3 and the continued ministry of the apostles in Jerusalem. Acts 2:42 and 3:1, as well as 4:1, make it clear that daily preaching, teaching, healing, and ministry in the temple area were a part of the apostles' daily routine.

On one such occasion, Peter and John were confronted by a man crippled from birth. Peter "helped him up, and instantly the man's feet and ankles became strong. He jumped to his feet and began to walk" (3:7–8). The crippled man's healing brought "wonder and amazement" to the crowd (3:10). Without hesitation, Peter credited Jesus Christ of Nazareth, the One they had handed over to be killed, as the One who had "given this complete healing" (3:16).

Peter was not gentle in speaking to the onlookers about their actions toward God's glorified servant, Jesus: "You killed the author of life, but God raised him from the dead" (3:15); "you acted in ignorance, as did your leaders" (3:17). With these indictments, Peter called his listeners to "Repent, then, and turn to God, so that your sins may be wiped out" (3:19). This risen Jesus is the Messiah promised from "all the prophets from Samuel on" (3:24). They (and we) are the heirs of these promises, and the covenant God made to Abraham (3:25).

Consider the themes of the apostles' messages following Pentecost:

- The firm confidence that Jesus of Nazareth was the one spoken of by Joel, David, Samuel, and the other prophets; that Jesus was the fulfillment of prophecy and the promise made to father Abraham.
- The accusation that the listeners were responsible for Jesus death' on the cross through their actions.
- The certainty that this same Jesus is now resurrected and sits at the right hand of God in heaven.
- That Jesus' promised Holy Spirit provides the disciples' boldness.

These themes, spoken without hesitation by the twelve apostles, were received with enthusiasm by the people. But not all were thrilled, for as we see in chapter 4, Peter and John were called to the Jewish high court to explain their actions.

The Arrest of Peter and John (Acts 4:1–4)

On yet another post-Pentecost day, **Peter and John** were found **speaking to the people** (v. 1). **It was evening** (v. 3). While they were speaking, a disturbance was brewing among **the priests and the captain of the temple guard and the Sadducees**

(v. 1). The **priests** and **Sadducees** were disturbed by what was being said. The **captain of the temple guard** was disturbed by the crowds and the potential ruckus that might occur as a result of this large mass of people.

WORDS FROM WESLEY

Acts 4:1

*And as they were speaking to the people, the priests—came upon them—*So wisely did God order, that they should first bear a full testimony to the truth in the temple, and then in the great council; to which they could have had no access, had they not been brought before it as criminals. (ENNT)

The priests had been a continuing frustration to Jesus and His disciples. They constantly questioned their teachings and seemingly lacked the observance of the Mosaic laws. The captain of the temple guard ranked next to the high priest in terms of authority. His charge was to ensure that order was maintained in the temple region. Neither the Romans nor the religious leaders wanted discord among the people that might demonstrate Jewish insurrection or stifle the privileged role the religious leaders had among the Romans for ensuring peace.

The Sadducees had theological grounds upon which to voice their objections. **They were greatly disturbed because the apostles were . . . proclaiming in Jesus the resurrection of the dead** (v. 2). The Sadducees saw the Pentateuch as taking precedence over the prophets and writings of the Old Testament. They rejected doctrines based in the oral tradition, such as the existence of spirits and angels, immortality, and the bodily resurrection.

The Pharisees, on the other hand, embraced the doctrine of resurrection. They were more favorably disposed theologically to the teachings of Christianity and based much of their teaching in oral tradition. It is interesting that during Jesus' life He sparred extensively with the Pharisees, and now post-resurrection, we find the apostles sparring with the Sadducees.

●

WORDS FROM WESLEY

Acts 4:2

The priests being grieved—That the name of Jesus was preached to the people; especially they were offended at the doctrine of His resurrection; for as they had put Him to death, His rising again proved Him to be the Just One, and so brought *his blood upon their heads*. The priests were grieved, lest their office and temple services should decline, and Christianity take root, through the preaching of the apostles, and their power of working miracles. (ENNT)

They seized Peter and John, and because it was evening, they put them in jail until the next day (v. 3). It was unlawful to call the Sanhedrin to meet at night, so Peter and John needed to be confined until a trial could be arranged. This incarceration, because of the message preached, is the first of several imprisonments recorded in Acts.

Regardless of the religious leaders' actions, the damage had been done. **Many who heard the message believed** (v. 4), and the response was large, with **the number of men** who believed growing **to about five thousand** (v. 4). It is unclear whether this five thousand was in addition to the three thousand recorded earlier (2:41) or if it was a cumulative number. Regardless, the numbers were growing, and this did not include women and children. No doubt this rapid growth concerned the religious leaders and thus led to the apostles' arrest.

The Interrogation before the Sanhedrin (Acts 4:5–12)

The next day the Sanhedrin **met in Jerusalem** (v. 5). This was the Senate and Supreme Court of the Jewish nation. Its membership of seventy was mainly Sadducees but included some Pharisees. The high priest served as president. For the apostles to appear before this austere group was a miracle in itself, lending credibility to their message, though they came as criminals.

In addition to **the rulers, elders and teachers of the law** (v. 5), **Annas the high priest was there, and so were Caiaphas, John, Alexander and the other men of the high priest's family** (v. 6). **Annas** was the former high priest, who was followed by his son-in-law **Caiaphas**, the current high priest. These men had tried Jesus only eight weeks before.

Little is known with certainty about John and Alexander. Bible scholar William Barclay explained who **the other men of the high priest's family** were. The priestly families, often called the chief priests, consisted of two groups. First were the ex-high priests, who were frequently deposed by the Romans, unlike the hereditary and priest-for-life status generally maintained in the Jewish culture. The second group were the extended families of those hereditary high priest families who garnered special prestige.

When Peter and John arrived, they were asked a battery of questions, but only one is recorded by Luke: **By what power or what name did you do this?** (v. 7). They questioned not whether a miracle had been performed, such was evident before many witnesses, but rather by whose authority this miracle had been performed. The authority of the Sanhedrin itself was being challenged, and that was not taken lightly.

Then Peter, who earlier in the courtyard had denied Christ but was now filled with the Holy Spirit, addressed the religious leaders with respect: **"Rulers and elders of the people!"** (v. 8). Peter's response was not in his own spirit, but the verb here indicates this was a special moment of inspiration from the Holy Spirit. Peter minced no words, but endeavored to tell the complete account of the **act of kindness shown to a cripple** (v. 9), giving credit to Jesus: "This account today **is by the name of Jesus Christ of Nazareth**. It is because of Him **that this man stands before you** completely **healed**. The credit is not to men, but to the one **you crucified but whom God raised from the dead**" (v. 10). Note here the Christ-centered theme of Peter's argument, similar to that of his sermon in 2:14–36.

WORDS FROM WESLEY

Acts 4:10

Be it known to you all—Probably the herald of God proclaimed this with a loud voice. *Whom God hath raised from the dead*—They knew in their own consciences that it was so. And though they had hired the soldiers to tell a most senseless and incredible tale to the contrary (Matt. 28:12, 15), yet it is observable, they did not, so far as we can learn, dare to plead it before Peter and John. (ENNT)

Peter was asked to defend his actions, but he went on the offensive. He quoted Psalm 118:22, one of the earliest messianic testimonies. Jesus is the Messiah, and clearly, **salvation is found in no one else, for there is no other name under heaven given to men by which we must be saved** (Acts 4:12). Jesus brings complete salvation, not merely physical healing, but healing from the sickness of sin. Everything related to salvation is tied up in this one individual who is **the stone you builders rejected** (v. 11).

The Sanhedrin Consulted (Acts 4:13–17)

The Sanhedrin was impressed by the courage of Peter and John. They **realized that they were unschooled, ordinary men**

(v. 13). These were not seminary-trained individuals who had been formally schooled as the rabbis. They were fishermen, lay theologians, but they **had been with Jesus** (v. 13), receiving direct instruction from Him. Jesus, too, though He lacked formal rabbinic education, had taught with similar authority.

The Sanhedrin **conferred** in closed session (v. 15). How could Luke have known what occurred during this closed session? He must have been informed by someone present. We are aware that some of the Sanhedrin were sympathetic to Jesus' message, and possibly they later shared the contents of that session.

The physical healing of the cripple could not be denied, for they could see the man standing with them. He was miraculously healed after suffering from birth as a cripple for over forty years (v. 22), but now **there was nothing they could say** (v. 14). What would they do with these men? **Everybody living in Jerusalem** had heard about the miracle that could not be denied (v. 16). But no law had been broken, religious or otherwise. It would not have been wise politically to punish them and further incite the people; but to simply free them without admonition would have shown weakness.

They decided to stop this thing from spreading any further in hopes of avoiding any undermining of their religious authority and bringing the wrath of the Romans. They chose to warn the disciples **to speak no longer to anyone in this name** (v. 17). They reasoned that if they threatened hard enough with more serious consequences, the men would stop.

Notice the Sanhedrin did not attempt to discredit either the healing of the cripple or the message the apostles were preaching—the resurrection of Jesus. This would have been an opportune time to render false the apostles' central affirmation of the risen Christ. If the resurrection argument could have been shown to be unfounded and incorrect, the apostles and the growing church would have met their demise. But no evidence was produced to counter the argument of the resurrection.

The Verdict (Acts 4:18–20)

Peter and John were called in and the verdict rendered: **they . . . commanded them not to speak or teach at all in the name of Jesus** (v. 18). Neither public nor private speaking was permissible. Again, note that the prohibition was not due to teaching lies, heresy, or inciting danger, but because the preaching was in the name of Jesus.

But from a clear conscience that recognized the truth and held it close by conviction of heart and mind, Peter replied, **"Judge for yourselves whether it is right in God's sight to obey you rather than God. For we cannot help speaking about what we have seen and heard"** (vv. 19–20). Peter and John were witnesses and could not dismiss what they knew to be true. How would the Sanhedrin judge the necessity of such a response to the truth? The apostles knew they must follow the divine command at all costs. They had no choice but to obey the truth.

WORDS FROM WESLEY

Acts 4:19

Whether it be just to obey you rather than God, judge ye— Was it not by the same spirit, that Socrates, when they were condemning him to death, for teaching the people, said, "O ye Athenians, I embrace and love you; but I will *obey God rather than you.* And if you would spare my life on condition I should cease to teach my fellow-citizens, I would die a thousand times rather than accept the proposal." (ENNT)

The response of Christians today must be the same. We must say and do what is right in God's sight, and we must speak and teach about what we have seen and heard and know to be true. Truth must be the natural outflow of the believer's life. When we are empowered by the Holy Spirit, as were Peter and John, we have nothing to fear before authorities, strangers, friends, and family. God's Spirit compels us to witness to the truth of the risen Savior.

DISCUSSION

History demonstrates that persecution grows strong Christians and multiplies their numbers.

1. Read Acts 4:1–2. Why do you think the proclamation of Jesus' resurrection was so disturbing to the priests and Sadducees?

2. Peter and John were imprisoned. Why do you agree or disagree that persecution befalls every believer who shares the gospel?

3. What encouragement for sharing the gospel do you find in verse 4?

4. Read Acts 3:1–10. Why did the miracle of a crippled man challenge the Sanhedrin's authority?

5. Read Acts 4:8–12. Why do you agree or disagree that Peter's words to the Sanhedrin demonstrated great courage?

6. How would you answer someone who claims salvation can be obtained by sincere devotion to one's religion?

7. Why do you agree or disagree that God can use a Spirit-filled poorly educated believer in a mighty way?

8. How should Christians respond if the government passed a law against evangelizing fellow citizens?

PRAYER

Father, please draw us nearer to You every day that we might shine with a light that shows we've been with You. Then give us the strength to boldly proclaim Your gospel through our actions and words.

HELPING BELIEVERS GROW

Acts 4:32–37; 11:19–26; 13:1–3

The Bible instructs believers to encourage
Christians to remain faithful.

It is said that when Sir Walter Scott was a boy, a teacher made him sit in a classroom corner and wear a dunce cap. When he was a young teen, he was in a house where literary guests were present. Scotland's revered poet Robert Burns was admiring a painting on which a couplet had been written. He asked the assembled guests if they knew who had written the couplet, but none did. Except young Walter, who whispered the author's name and quoted the rest of the poem.

"Ah, bairnie," Burns told Walter, "ye will be a great mon yet in Scotland some day!" That encouragement inspired Sir Walter Scott to become Scotland's most prolific novelist.

This study summons every believer to be an encourager.

COMMENTARY

God always provides what His church needs. One can often see what a church needs by the people God brings in its doors. The gifts and talents new believers bring to the body say a lot about what God knows a particular congregation needs. This dynamic is seen in the early church.

The Holy Spirit had been poured out on the day of Pentecost. The early church went from just over a hundred to three thousand people in one day. By Acts 4, the church was at least five thousand and growing. The rapid growth, the miracles, and the teaching of the apostles disturbed the religious establishment, so they took action. Peter and John were arrested and imprisoned overnight.

In the morning, these apostles were hauled in front of the ruling religious tribunal. Peter and John did not defend themselves. They spoke about Jesus. When the tribunal "saw the courage of Peter and John and realized that they were unschooled, ordinary men, they were astonished and they took note that these men had been with Jesus" (Acts 4:13).

What do unschooled, ordinary men need when they are called to lead a new, exploding, multiethnic megachurch that is at odds with the government? Among other things, they need courage. How did God provide for this ongoing need? He sent a man named Joseph. We are introduced to Joseph at the end of Acts 4.

Encouragement through Action (Acts 4:32–37)

Not everyone in a church of five thousand people knew the apostles personally. But Joseph stood out in a crowd. Joseph came from a good Jewish family. He had grown up outside of Israel on the island of **Cyprus** and was a **Levite** (v. 36). He would have been schooled in Jewish Law and able to carry out the duties of a priest. The apostles knew Joseph well enough to give him a nickname: **Barnabas**, meaning **Son of Encouragement** (v. 36). The name stuck. Hereafter, in the Bible and this study, Joseph is called Barnabas.

According to the *American Heritage Dictionary*, the word *encouragement* means "to inspire with hope, courage, or confidence." The Greek word here also has overtones of comfort. Barnabas was one who brought courage, hope, confidence, and comfort to the apostles and the church. This is what the church needed in a time of expansion and persecution.

The believers in the early church lived in community. What they owned, they believed was owned by the whole community of believers (v. 32). The apostles did not mandate this (5:4). The believers shared their possessions because they believed this was the appropriate expression of love in their circumstances.

WORDS FROM WESLEY

Acts 4:34

Neither was there any one among them that wanted—We may observe, this is added as the proof that *great grace was upon them all*. And it was the immediate, necessary consequence of it: yea, and must be to the end of the world. In all ages and nations, the same cause, the same degree of grace, could not but in like circumstances produce the same effect. *For whosoever were possessors of houses and lands sold them*—Not that there was any particular command for this; but there was great grace and great love: of which this was the natural fruit. (ENNT)

There was a likelihood that they would be persecuted for their faith. They could be thrown out of temple. They could be ostracized from their families. They could lose their means of making a living in this Jewish city. How does one have the courage to face that kind of persecution? It comes from a community willing to stand behind its people. A community like this inspires hope; it inspires courage. But communities need leaders. While the apostles were that kind of leader, they were set apart from the rest of the community because of who they were. The community needed leaders to arise from within.

Barnabas became one of those leaders. He came from within the community. He led the way and inspired courage. Barnabas **owned . . . a field** (4:37). As a Levite, he was not supposed to own land within Israel. So this property was likely either outside Israel or it came to him through his wife's family. He took this property, sold it, and brought the money to the apostles. He put the money **at the apostles' feet** (v. 37). This was an indication that the money was under the authority of the apostles. In this way, Barnabas affirmed the apostles in their leadership.

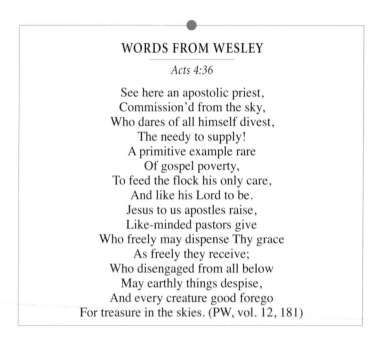

WORDS FROM WESLEY

Acts 4:36

See here an apostolic priest,
Commission'd from the sky,
Who dares of all himself divest,
The needy to supply!
A primitive example rare
Of gospel poverty,
To feed the flock his only care,
And like his Lord to be.
Jesus to us apostles raise,
Like-minded pastors give
Who freely may dispense Thy grace
As freely they receive;
Who disengaged from all below
May earthly things despise,
And every creature good forego
For treasure in the skies. (PW, vol. 12, 181)

Encouragement can come in many forms. Sometimes appropriate words spoken at an appropriate time can bring encouragement. But actions like those of Barnabas tend to speak louder than words. This action raised Barnabas's standing in the community. In Acts 5, Ananias and Sapphira wanted this same standing without the same cost. They sold a piece of land and pretended to put all the money from that sale at the apostles' feet. The only reason they would do that is to receive the same accolades that came to Barnabas.

Saul, who would become the apostle Paul, had persecuted the church. He had Christians arrested and imprisoned and perhaps even cheered at their executions. The early church was afraid of Saul. But as we previously studied, God met Saul on the road to

Damascus, where Saul was wonderfully converted. While Christians in Damascus knew of the change, Christians in Jerusalem were not ready to welcome Saul into the fellowship of believers. Enter Barnabas, a man of courage. He got to know Saul. He heard the story of the church in Damascus. Then he introduced Saul to the apostles.

People who are real encouragers tend to inspire confidence. Their judgment carries weight. Saul was accepted into the fellowship of the church because of Barnabas's introduction.

Encouragers Affirm People (Acts 11:19–26)

Remember that the early church was almost exclusively made up of Jewish believers. The message of the gospel that explained that Jesus was the Messiah thrilled these believers. The message that the full requirements of the law were fulfilled in Jesus amazed these believers. The knowledge that Jesus was the Lamb of God who took away the sins of the world and that no other sacrifice was needed caused their hearts to break out in worship. But concepts like the Messiah, law, and sacrifices were all Jewish. So these believers were incredulous at the thought that Jesus could have come for people who were not Jewish.

WORDS FROM WESLEY

Acts 11:20

Some of them were men of Cyprus and Cyrene—Who were mere accustomed to converse with the Gentiles. *Who coming into Antioch*—Then the capital of Syria, and next Rome and Alexandria, the most considerable city of the empire. *Spake to the Greeks*—As the Greeks were the most celebrated of the Gentile nations near Judea, the Jews called all the Gentiles by that name. Here we have the first account of the preaching the Gospel to the idolatrous Gentiles. All those to whom it had been preached before, did at least worship one God, the God of Israel. (ENNT)

When persecution went from a possibility to a reality in Jerusalem, believers spread over the then-known world. As they moved from city to city, they told people about Jesus. Most of them told only Jewish people (v. 19). But **some** who had grown up among the Gentiles started to tell the **Greeks** of the city of **Antioch** about Jesus (v. 20).

The Lord blessed their efforts. **A great number of** Greeks **believed** (v. 21). These were not the first Gentile conversions (see Acts 10:24), but Antioch was the first Gentile church. News of this church reached the church in Jerusalem. It was difficult for the Jerusalem church to wrap its mind around the fact that Jesus came for Greek people, as well. The Greeks didn't know anything about the laws of God. They were unfamiliar with the covenants of God. It was one thing for pious Gentiles to come to faith, but the church in Antioch was not made up of pious Gentiles. It was made up of normal Greek people.

The Jerusalem church had to investigate, so they commissioned **Barnabas** to go **to Antioch** (v. 22). Barnabas was the perfect person, since he had demonstrated leadership and humility. He had demonstrated courage in taking steps toward Saul. He had grown up in Cyprus and understood the Greek mind. But he was a Levite—Jewish to the core.

Barnabas arrived in Antioch and witnessed the blessing of the Lord. People were believing in and following Jesus. What does one do in a place where God is at work? What Barnabas did: he used his spiritual gift. **When he arrived and saw the evidence of the grace of God, he was glad and encouraged them all to remain true to the Lord with all their hearts** (v. 23). Barnabas instilled hope, courage, and confidence in that early church. He encouraged them toward wholehearted devotion to Jesus. He affirmed the people in what the Lord was doing among them.

It cannot be overstated how outside the box a Greek church was for those early Jewish believers. However, when God moves, He often demolishes our preconceptions. It takes a person of character to move with God in these times. Luke spelled out Barnabas's character: **He was a good man, full of the Holy Spirit and faith** (v. 24).

Barnabas was a **good man**. He was able to see past his prejudice to what God was doing. He was able to set aside his agenda for God's agenda. He was able to keep from imposing his culture on the work of God. Only people who have good hearts are able to move with God in this way.

He was **full of the Holy Spirit**. All the believers were filled with the Spirit in the book of Acts. However, this description of Barnabas seems to set him apart from the average believer. Stephen is the only other believer in the book of Acts to whom this description is ascribed. Paul indicated we should continually be filled with the Spirit (Eph. 5:18). The reason we need to be continually filled is that we often leak. Barnabas seems to have stopped the leaks.

He also was full of **faith** (Acts 11:24). He was able to believe God for great things. He was able to believe in the goodness of the grace of God in situations where others would be unable to see what God was doing.

The fact that Barnabas was all these things allowed God to use him to strengthen the church. But it also allowed God to use him to see many people come to know the Lord. Verse 24 says, **a great number of people were brought to the Lord.** Barnabas shows us that character matters. Barnabas's character shows up again in his next action. When he saw all the people who needed to be discipled, he recognized his limitations. So Barnabas went looking for Saul in Tarsus. When he found Saul, he brought him to Antioch. There both Saul and Barnabas discipled the church for a whole year (Acts 11:26). People of character know their limits.

Barnabas Continued in Ministry (Acts 13:1–3)

Barnabas seemed to have become the senior pastor of the church at Antioch. The leadership was obviously shared, but Barnabas seems to have been an essential part of the leadership. Verse 1 doesn't tell us if Barnabas was a prophet or teacher, but it indicates that he was one or the other.

The Spirit of God came upon the church meeting. **The Holy Spirit** spoke and **said, "Set apart for me Barnabas and Saul for the work to which I have called them"** (v. 2). The church **prayed** for them **and sent them off** (v. 3). This sent Saul and Barnabas on their first missionary trip together. This missionary journey was not only a change for Barnabas; it was also a change for the church at Antioch.

WORDS FROM WESLEY

Acts 13:2

Separate me Barnabas and Saul for the work to which I have called them—This was not ordaining them. St. Paul was ordained long before, and that *not of men, neither by man:* it was only inducting him to the province for which our Lord had appointed him from the beginning, and which was now revealed to the prophets and teachers. In consequence of this they fasted, prayed, and laid their hands on them, a rite which was used not in ordination only, but in blessing, and on many other occasions. (ENNT)

Barnabas was the one who confirmed, affirmed, and validated the ministry at Antioch. Under his leadership, many people were won to Christ. Barnabas brought in the appropriate people so this church could be discipled. The church had sat under Barnabas's teaching. Now he was leaving.

As a good leader, Barnabas had other leadership in place. When God called Barnabas and Saul, there was no fear in the church. There was a commissioning and a sending. This speaks to the strength of Barnabas's leadership. We know Saul/Paul better than we know Barnabas, because he penned many of the letters in the New Testament. But Barnabas seemed to have been more influential than Saul/Paul in the early church. His influence came through his spiritual gifts. He was an encourager. He demonstrated this gift in action and words. Barnabas's influence was extended because he was a man of good character. He rose in the church to become a leader. His leadership put the early Gentile church on a strong foundation.

DISCUSSION

Aren't there wonderful helpers in your church? Doesn't it seem that God has placed them there to encourage others at the right times and in the right ways? First-century believers received help too, especially from Barnabas.

1. According to Acts 4:36, the apostles nicknamed Joseph "Barnabas," meaning "Son of Encouragement." If other Christians wanted to give you a nickname that reflected your ministry, what would you want it to be? Why?

2. How has a believer encouraged you in some significant way?

3. How might you encourage other believers in nonverbal ways?

4. Read Acts 9:26–27. Specifically, how did Barnabas alleviate his fellow believers' fears about Saul?

5. What evidence of racial or religious pride do you observe in Acts 11:19?

6. According to Acts 11:20–22, how did the church at Jerusalem demonstrate full confidence in Barnabas?

7. Why do you agree or disagree that holiness and racial (or any) prejudice are mutually exclusive?

8. Read Acts 11:24 and 13:1–2. Would you have liked to sit under Barnabas's teaching at Antioch? Why or why not?

9. Read Acts 13:3. How might your church encourage its members to be actively involved in missions?

PRAYER

Father, please make us people of encouragement and grace, and show us who we can uplift and how to do it. Teach us Your Word and how to apply it that we may live in Your wisdom.

6

A FULLY SURRENDERED LIFE

Acts 6:8–15; 7:51—8:1

A fully surrendered life powerfully reveals God.

Communist bandits poured into a Chinese village in 1934 and seized missionaries John and Betty Stamm. They tied the young couple's wrists and forced them into a tiny hut, where they spent the last night of their lives. The next morning the bandits murdered John and Betty. When word of their martyrdom reached the West, numerous young men and women dedicated their lives for missionary service.

While in the hut, John wrote: "My wife, baby, and myself are today in the hands of communist bandits. Whether we will be released or not, no one knows. May God be magnified in our bodies, whether by life or by death. Philippians 1:20."

This study begs the question: Are you willing to lay down your life for the Lord?

COMMENTARY

The young Jerusalem church, made up almost exclusively of Jews, experienced considerable opposition from within the wider Jewish community, most notably from its ruling council, the Sanhedrin. This was the same body responsible for bringing Jesus to trial and demanding His execution at the hands of the Romans. The Sanhedrin of seventy-one religious leaders, led by the high priest, was dominated by a priestly aristocracy known as the Sadducees, a religious sect loyal to the law of Moses but opposed to the oral tradition of the Pharisees. Peter and John had been brought before the Sanhedrin after preaching to the crowds in the vicinity of the temple, and the leaders commanded them not to teach or preach any longer in the name of Jesus (Acts 4:1–21). All the apostles were later arrested for preaching in Jesus' name and brought before the Sanhedrin. The members of the Sanhedrin wanted to kill them but were fearful of what the people would do, so they had them flogged and warned them yet again not to speak in the name of Jesus (Acts 5:27–40).

The church grew rapidly, and along with growth came a number of problems. One of those was the apparent neglect of the Greek-speaking widows in the church's daily food distribution ministry. There was a significant group of Jewish people within Jerusalem whose native tongue was Greek (Hellenists). They had grown up in other regions of the Greek world, but now made their home in Jerusalem. A sizeable number of these non-Aramaic-speaking Jews were converted at Pentecost. Whether the neglect of the widows within the church was due to ethnic or cultural bias is unclear, but the church's answer to this problem was the selection of seven deacons who would oversee the food distribution ministry and allow the apostles to continue to devote themselves to prayer and the ministry of the Word. Among those seven deacons—all Greek-speaking Hellenists themselves—was Stephen, who was known to be full of the Holy Spirit, wisdom, and faith (Acts 6:3, 5).

Stephen Engaged in Evangelistic Ministry (Acts 6:8–10)

Although he had been chosen by the apostles as a deacon to wait on tables (Acts 6:2), Stephen had additional spiritual gifts. He was **a man** who was **full of God's grace and power**, and he used his gifts to do **great wonders and miraculous signs among the people** (v. 8). This tied his ministry to that of the apostles and to Christ. He was the first non-apostle mentioned as performing miracles and also the first non-apostle whose sermon is recorded (7:2–53). His ministry caught the attention of a group of Jews from the **Synagogue of the Freedmen** (6:8) who were residing in Jerusalem but were from Cyrene and Alexandria in Africa and the provinces of Cilicia and Asia. Possibly Stephen, as a Greek-speaking Jew, had been a part of this group before coming to Christ.

A few **members of** this **Synagogue . . . began to argue with Stephen** (v. 9). It is uncertain what the nature of this argument was, but Stephen showed himself a capable debater—so much that his opponents **could not stand up against his wisdom or the Spirit by whom he spoke** (v. 10). These were the two qualities the apostles had used in their selection process of Stephen and the other six deacons (6:3).

WORDS FROM WESLEY

Acts 6:8

One single minister renew'd
And fill'd with faith's resistless might,
Does wonders in the cause of God,
Puts Satan's synagogue to flight,
In all his loving toils succeeds,
And Christ among the people spreads.
Such ministry, O Christ ordain,
And fill with power invincible
Thy truth and goodness to maintain
Through *Stephen's* faith, and fervent zeal
Mighty the alien host to' o'erthrow,
And all Thy gracious wonders show. (PW, vol. 12, 199)

Stephen Was Arrested and Brought before the Sanhedrin (Acts 6:11–15)

When the members of the Synagogue of the Freedmen were unable to win their arguments with Stephen, they resorted to slander as they began to stir up the people with accusations about his teaching. **They secretly persuaded some men to say, "We have heard Stephen speak words of blasphemy against Moses and against God"** (v. 11). These accusations, the same that had been leveled at Jesus, were inflammatory but blatantly false. They were also hard to prove and harder to refute.

The opposition against Stephen began to snowball as his opponents continued to stir up the people, the elders, and the teachers of the law. These latter two groups had significant influence among the religious hierarchy, so **they seized Stephen and brought him before the Sanhedrin** (v. 12).

Stephen's opponents managed to find people who were willing to testify against them before the Sanhedrin. They were false witnesses, but they still accused Stephen of **speaking against this holy place and against the law** (v. 13). Their accusations were probably half-truths—as they had been when Jesus was accused before their body. Jesus had said the temple would be destroyed, but He was speaking about the temple of His body. He had also said He had come to fulfill the law of Moses, not to change the customs Moses handed down. It is possible that Stephen's words were similarly twisted.

WORDS FROM WESLEY
Acts 6:15

As the face of an angel—Covered with supernatural lustre. They reckoned his preaching of Jesus to be the Christ, was destroying Moses and the law; and God bears witness to him, with the same glory as He did to Moses, when He gave the law by him. (ENNT)

While the witnesses were testifying against him, **all who were sitting in the Sanhedrin looked intently at Stephen** (v. 15).

They undoubtedly wanted to know what his reaction would be. Yet instead of seeing a man who feared the trial's outcome, they saw a man whose **face was like the face of an angel** (v. 15). Like Moses when he came down from Sinai after being with the Lord, Stephen's face was a glowing reflection of God's glory.

Stephen's Defense Angered His Accusers (Acts 7:51–53)

The high priest looked at Stephen and asked him if the charges against him were true. This was his moment. Jesus had told His disciples the day would come when they would be "delivered to synagogues and prisons" and brought before kings and governors on account of His name. In that day, they would become His witnesses, but they were not to worry about how they should defend themselves, for they would be given words and wisdom none of their adversaries would be able to resist or contradict (Luke 21:12–15).

Stephen spoke eloquently. He began by reciting Israel's history from the time of Abraham through the patriarchs and Moses to the time of Solomon's building of the temple. He noted how their forefathers had a history of disobedience to the law. There was nothing in his speech the council could disagree with or use against him. Yet Stephen had unusual boldness as he told the story, especially when he looked straight at the members of the Sanhedrin and said, **"You stiff-necked people, with uncircumcised hearts and ears! You are just like your fathers"** (Acts 7:51).

Those were fighting words. Stephen threw down the gauntlet. But he was not finished. He told them they always resisted the Holy Spirit and that their fathers had persecuted every prophet, even those who predicted the coming of the righteous One. Jeremiah, Isaiah, Amos, and many others had experienced persecution because of their message. Now, though, it was not their fathers who were on trial, but they themselves, as Stephen said, **"And**

now you have betrayed and murdered him" (v. 52). Stephen was on trial for rejecting the law of Moses, but it was he who put his accusers on trial for having received the law and refusing to obey it.

Stephen Became the Church's First Martyr (Acts 7:54—8:1)

The Sanhedrin did not take Stephen's words lightly. Peter had accused them of the same things (Acts 3:13–15), but Stephen's words stung even harder. **They were furious and gnashed their teeth at him** (7:54). In the midst of the council's anger, Stephen remained calm. He had been chosen to serve the church as a deacon because he was a man known to be full of the Holy Spirit. Nowhere was that fact more evident than here in his moment of trial. The Spirit had given him the words. Now the Spirit was giving him a vision of what was to come and the strength to look past the moment to the glory that awaited.

Stephen looked toward heaven and announced, **"I see heaven open and the Son of Man standing at the right hand of God"** (v. 56). The Scriptures are clear that Christ's posture after finishing His work of redemption is to be seated at the right hand of his Father (Ps. 110:1; Mark 14:62; Heb. 1:3; 12:2). But Stephen saw Jesus standing at God's right hand, as if to give approval and commendation for the witness he had just borne (Luke 12:8) and ready to receive His faithful servant home.

When Stephen said this, the members of the council **covered their ears** (Acts 7:57). It was more than they could bear. In a moment of passion, they screamed **at the top of their voices . . . rushed at him, dragged him out of the city and began to stone him** (vv. 57–58). Stoning was an Old Testament punishment for serious offenses against the character of God or the Hebrew community. But sentence was not pronounced in this case, nor did the Sanhedrin have authority to execute people. (Jesus was handed over to the Roman authorities for that purpose.) It appears this was more a mob action, incited by what they felt were the inflammatory words of Stephen.

WORDS FROM WESLEY

Acts 7:58

The witnesses laid down their clothes at the feet of a young man, whose name was Saul—O Saul, couldst thou have believed, if one had told thee, that thou thyself shouldst be stoned in the same cause? And shouldst triumph in committing thy soul likewise to that Jesus whom thou art now blaspheming? His dying prayer reached thee, as well as many others. And the martyr Stephen, and Saul the persecutor (afterward his brother both in faith and martyrdom) are now joined in everlasting friendship, and dwell together in the happy company of those who *have made their robes white in the blood of the Lamb.* (ENNT)

While the mob was stoning him, Stephen still had a few brief moments to pray. In those moments his prayer was similar to that of Jesus while on the cross (Luke 23:46): **"Lord Jesus, receive my spirit"** (Acts 7:59). He had seen Jesus standing at God's right hand and waiting for him. Now he knew his time had come. But, like Jesus (Luke 23:34), he forgave his persecutors, saying, **"Lord, do not hold this sin against them"** (Acts 7:60). He had learned from his Master important lessons about how to live and how to die. When he died, the text says simply that **he fell asleep** (v. 60).

Meanwhile, something else was taking place along the sidelines. Those who were stoning Stephen **laid their clothes at the feet of a young man named Saul** (v. 58). This is the first mention of him. Possibly he had been a member of the Synagogue of the Freedmen who brought Stephen before the Sanhedrin (he was from Tarsus in Cilicia). Even though he did not pick up stones to throw, he **was there, giving approval to** Stephen's

death (8:1), a fact Saul/Paul later acknowledged in his report of the incident (22:20). Luke included this fact to indicate Stephen's death was not in vain. His death made a profound impact on this young man named Saul (later, Paul), whom the Lord would later use to evangelize a significant portion of the Gentile world.

WORDS FROM WESLEY

Acts 8:1

At that time there was great persecution against the church— Their adversaries having tasted blood, were the more eager. *And they were all dispersed—* Not all the church: if so, who would have remained for the apostles to teach, or Saul to persecute? But *all* the teachers *except the apostles*, who though in the most danger, stayed with the flock. (ENNT)

DISCUSSION

Anyone who has been called out knows what an unpleasant experience it is. But wouldn't it be far more unpleasant to be dragged into court by a hateful mob to face false charges? That's what happened to Stephen, a leader in the early church.

1. Read Acts 6:1–7. How did the apostles address the complaint raised by Grecian Jews?

2. Why do you agree or disagree that the pastoral staff should handle every complaint that arises?

3. Read Acts 6:8–9. Why would opposition arise against someone who was "full of grace and power"?

4. What sort of trouble do you think people might cause a pastor if they can't tolerate his or her wise Bible teaching?

5. Read Acts 7:1–53. How would you summarize Stephen's defense before the Sanhedrin?

6. In your opinion, why does the truth anger some people?

7. When he was being stoned to death, Stephen saw Jesus. Why do you think Jesus was standing at God's right hand?

8. Why do you agree or disagree that the Holy Spirit can fill your heart with forgiveness for those who mistreat you?

9. Read Acts 8:1. How do you think Stephen's martyrdom affected Saul?

PRAYER

Father, give us boldness to speak Your truth, always with love, regardless of the repercussions. Help us to be so close to You that we instantly sense Your presence at our times of greatest need.

SELFLESS MINISTRY

Acts 8:9–25

Allowing the Holy Spirit to reveal our motives is
imperative to victorious Christian living and ministry.

A small church wanted to reach out to people in the
neighborhood, but nothing seemed to attract the neighbors to
church. One day, however, the church learned that a number of
cheap motels not far from the church housed men and women
who were involved in a prison work-release program. Some
church members were reluctant to invite ex-cons to church. They
worried that their children might not be safe. A few objected,
"Those people are not our kind." However, a few members
blitzed the motels, drove work-release participants to church,
and treated them to dinner after church.

This study challenges us to get out of our comfort zone and
minister to people who seem to be different from us.

COMMENTARY

The stoning of Stephen and the persecution of the church in
Jerusalem set the stage for God to dramatically expand the ministry
of the church. The fierce attacks on Christians in that city sent
believers scattering throughout Judea and Samaria. From a
human perspective, this dispersion would seem cruel, because
we focus on the suffering of God's people. But from God's
perspective, it was the beginning of something wonderful. Even
as seed is scattered to produce a harvest, so God scattered His
people to produce a greater crop that included Samaritans and
eventually Gentiles.

WORDS FROM WESLEY

Acts 8:4

In the eighth chapter we read, "There was a great persecution against the church which was at Jerusalem; and they were all scattered abroad throughout the regions of Judea and Samaria, except the apostles" (v. 1). "Therefore they that were scattered abroad, went everywhere preaching the word" (v. 4). . . . Here, then, is an undeniable proof, what was the practice of the apostolic age. Here you see not one, but a multitude of lay preachers, men that were only sent of God.

Indeed so far is the practice of the apostolic age from inclining us to think it was *unlawful* for a man to preach before he was ordained, that we have reason to think, it was then accounted *necessary*. (WJW, vol. 5, 488–489)

The Samaritans were hated by the Jews because they were half-breeds. They were the descendants of the Jews who had been carried off into the Assyrian captivity from the northern kingdom of Israel. These Jews had been assimilated into that culture and eventually intermarried, producing the Samaritans. Because Jews had no dealings with Samaritans, they had their own temple (John 4:9, 20) and forms of worship.

In Acts 6, we were introduced to seven men who were divinely chosen to be special servants to the church. One of these was Philip. Philip began as a deacon, but his ministry expanded and he became an effective evangelist (Acts 8:5). Philip, full of the Holy Spirit, was demonstrating the power of God through miraculous signs. He was casting out demons and healing the sick and handicapped (8:6–7).

God was moving the gospel from Jerusalem, the home of the Jews, to Samaria and eventually to the ends of the earth, just as Jesus promised before ascending to heaven (1:8). He was using surrendered vessels like Philip, who shared the power of God through preaching. But God also was using signs and wonders to bring credibility to that message.

Simon the Sorcerer (Acts 8:9–13)

Simon the sorcerer was a well-known man in Samaria. Scripture gives us a glimpse into what Simon was like. **He boasted that he was someone great** (v. 9). He had an exaggerated estimation of his importance. People from all stations and walks of life were noticing him and declaring, **"This man is the divine power known as the Great Power"** (v. 10). They saw him not only as doing great things, but being something special. This puffed him up all the more.

Simon **had amazed them for a long time with his magic** (v. 11). He was not the kind of magician who entertained with sleight of hand. Rather, his magic came from a practice known as sorcery. Sorcerers performed healings, cast out demons, and practiced astrology. Their power came not from God, but from Satan and his demonic realm. Simon was producing counterfeit signs and wonders. Simon's real goal was to build both a name and a treasury. He would receive large sums of money for his services.

Jesus told us these same "sorcerers" would be evident in the last days (2 Thess. 2:9). It is important that Christians are not drawn in by the miraculous without first testing to see what spirit is behind these signs. Jesus warned that even the elect would be deceived and drawn away (Matt. 24:24).

Early church fathers identified a man called Simon Magus who may have been this Simon. A sect of Gnosticism claimed Simon to be their follower. If this information is true, Simon never came to surrender completely to the living God, but continued to practice his magic and promote himself.

Those who manufacture counterfeits are acutely aware of the genuine when they see it. Such was the case for Simon. He must have been curious about Philip, who preached a new message — the gospel of Jesus Christ. He saw countless **men, women**, and children respond to this message and be **baptized** in **the name**

of Jesus (Acts 8:12). Scripture tells us Simon responded to the message **and was baptized** (v. 13).

WORDS FROM WESLEY
Acts 8:12

But when they believed—What Philip preached, then they saw and felt the real power of God, and submitted thereto. (ENNT)

He was enamored with this new message but even more curious about this new power. **He followed Philip everywhere, astonished by the great signs and miracles** (v. 13). It would seem that Simon did not believe in the Word of God, but in the miraculous signs. Because he was able to perform imitation signs, he was distracted by the out-workings of the Holy Spirit. Instead of these signs reinforcing his faith, they became his focus. Perhaps he never really responded to the message to repent and turn from his sins. Perhaps all he responded to was the desire to be a part of something greater than he was able to do himself.

The signs Philip performed brought glory to God, not to Philip. The signs Simon performed brought glory only to Simon. This desire to be noticed and important hindered Simon from completely responding to the gospel message.

The Holy Spirit (Acts 8:14–17)

Word reached Jerusalem about what God was doing in Samaria. The church leaders there **heard that Samaria had accepted the word of God,** so the church in Jerusalem **sent Peter and John** to check things out (v. 14). Jewish Christians were not sure whether non-Jews could receive the Holy Spirit.

Note that God slowly expanded His message. He moved from Jews to Samaritans, who were half-Jewish. He was beginning to help Jewish Christians to see the message of salvation was for all people, not just the Jews. It took Peter's encounter with Cornelius (Acts 10) to fully convince the Jews that the gospel was for Gentiles as well.

Evidently, the Samaritans had not received the Holy Spirit when they believed. **They had simply been baptized** in water **into the name of the Lord Jesus** (8:16). So when Peter and John **arrived, they prayed for them that they might receive the Holy Spirit** (v. 15).

There have been several explanations given as to why these Samaritan believers did not receive the Holy Spirit when they believed. Some have said it was necessary for Peter and John to come so the Samaritans would identify with the Jews instead of creating their own church and religious practices as they had done in the past. Some have offered that the Samaritans' faith was inadequate and that it took Peter and John laying **hands on** them to impart the Holy Spirit (v. 17). Others use this passage to support a second work of grace. In other words, the Samaritans needed an infilling of the Spirit that corresponded to the Jewish Pentecost. Still others believe Peter and John needed to see the Samaritans receive the Spirit just as they had, because only then could they give an eyewitness account to the mother church in Jerusalem.

Believers receive the *indwelling* Holy Spirit the moment they believe. However, everyone does not receive the *filling* of the Spirit at this point in his or her spiritual journey. The filling of the Spirit comes when we surrender ourselves to Christ and make Him Lord of our lives. Some people testify this comes at their initial experience with Christ. Others receive a second "touch" or "work of grace."

We cannot always figure out God's actions. The important thing to remember is that God does not have a formula He uses for every person. Everyone has his or her own special experience with the Lord. So let us be careful not to put down others whose experiences do not completely align with our own.

Evil Motives (Acts 8:18–25)

Simon had been mesmerized by the signs and wonders Philip performed. He was even more intrigued with the impartation of the Holy Spirit through the laying on of hands. He saw something he wanted for his own benefit and so **he offered them money and said, "Give me also this ability so that everyone on whom I lay my hands may receive the Holy Spirit"** (vv. 18–19). He saw this power as a business opportunity, not a spiritual experience. In fact, the term *simony*—the buying and selling of anything considered sacred—came from Simon's example.

The apostles not only discerned Simon's sin, but they sternly reprimanded him, saying, **"May your money perish with you, because you thought you could buy the gift of God with money! You have no part or share in this ministry, because your heart is not right before God"** (vv. 20–21). This was strong language, but Simon needed to hear this rebuke. There are times we can correct with a gentle spirit, but there are also times when correction must be done with power and authority.

WORDS FROM WESLEY

Acts 8:21

For thy heart is not right before God—Probably St. Peter discerned this, long before he had declared it; although it does not appear, that God gave to any of the apostles an universal power of discerning the hearts of all they conversed with; any more than an universal power of healing all the sick they came near. This we are sure St. Paul had not; though he was not inferior to the chief of the apostles. Otherwise he would not have suffered the illness of Epaphroditus to have brought him *so near to death* (Phil. 2:25–27). Nor have left so useful a fellow-labourer as *Trophimus sick at Miletus*, 2 Tim. 4:20. (ENNT)

Peter confronted Simon's erroneous thinking head-on. He could not let him continue to believe the gift of God was something that could be purchased. He called Simon to **repent of this** sin (v. 22). (Repentance means to change your mind and then reorder your life.) Simon didn't need a reconditioning of his old life, but a complete reconstruction.

WORDS FROM WESLEY
Acts 8:22

Repent—if perhaps the thought of thy heart may be forgiven thee—Without all doubt if he had repented, he would have been forgiven. The doubt was, Whether he would repent? *Thou art in the gall of bitterness*—In the highest degree of wickedness, which is bitterness, that is, misery to the soul; *and in the bond of iniquity*—Fast bound therewith. (ENNT)

Peter's words can lead us to believe that Simon had never truly given his heart to the Lord. He declared, **"I see that you are full of bitterness and captive to sin"** (v. 23). Salvation frees us from sin. It doesn't keep us captive to it (see Gal. 5:1). The word translated **bitterness** (Acts 8:23) literally means "poison." Evil motives had poisoned Simon's heart and were holding him prisoner to his sin.

Simon said to Peter, **"Pray to the Lord for me so that nothing you have said may happen to me"** (v. 24). Was this true repentance or simply a reaction of fear that something horrible was about to happen to him? Only God can truly judge the heart.

We must be aware that within our churches are counterfeit Christians who appear right on the outside, but whose hearts are full of themselves. We cannot judge them, for only God knows a person's heart. But we can examine ourselves to see if we are of faith (2 Cor. 13:5). We can repent of our sin and reorder our lives according to God's will for us as individuals. May the spirit of Simon be eradicated from the church in the last days. We desperately need the purging work of the Holy Spirit so we might become a people "having no spot or wrinkle" living "holy and blameless" before the Lord (Eph. 5:27 NASB).

Peter and John returned to Jerusalem but not without **preaching the gospel in many Samaritan villages** (Acts 8:25). These apostles began to understand that God was working among the Samaritans. They could have used the example of Simon as an excuse not to share. But Peter and John saw beyond one negative experience to the great things God was doing. Let us never lose heart in sharing the message of salvation. May we, too, look beyond our own feelings and negative experiences to what God wants to do through us. May we always be ready to give an answer for the hope that is in us (1 Pet. 3:15).

DISCUSSION

How would you feel if you believed God wanted you to leave the blessings of your church's fellowship and engage in a cross-cultural ministry away from home? He called Philip to do that very thing.

1. Read Acts 6:5. How was Philip equipped for ministry?

2. Read Acts 1:8 and 8:4–5. How did God move His witnesses out of Jerusalem?

3. Why do you agree or disagree that persecution of believers today would destroy the church?

4. Why should believers be very careful about attaching credibility to so-called miraculous signs?

5. Why do you agree or disagree that Simon the sorcerer was not genuinely converted to Christ?

6. How do you explain the difference between the Spirit's indwelling and His filling?

7. Why do you agree or disagree that some religious leaders are more interested in getting rich than in serving the Lord?

8. How did Peter and John's visit to Samaria help to connect the believers in Jerusalem with those in Samaria?

PRAYER

Father, please grant us the wisdom to discern those whose works come from You and those who are counterfeits. And show us where our motives may be selfish. Replace them with godly motives, that we may serve You with pure hearts.

BE PREPARED FOR GOD TO USE YOU

Acts 8:26–40

God works through us when we make ourselves available to Him.

A young Irishman flying from Ireland to Chicago sat next to a Christian, and the young man's life was changed forever. The Christian led the young man to the Lord and then invited him to live at his home in Chicago while he pursued his career there. Soon after settling into his host's home and church, the Irishman felt called to enter the ministry. He enrolled in a Bible college, became the youth pastor for his church, and studied to become a pastor. Today, he is back in Ireland serving as a pastor.

This study encourages us to follow the Lord's leading to share the good news with individuals, even if they are strangers from a different country or culture.

COMMENTARY

Acts 8 marks a transition in the early church. In chapters 1 through 7, the church was born, with the coming of the Holy Spirit at Pentecost, followed by the gospel being preached in Jerusalem. With chapter 8, the gospel began spreading beyond Jerusalem. This was as Jesus had commanded in Acts 1:8: "You will be my witnesses in Jerusalem, and in all Judea and Samaria, and to the ends of the earth." Philip, one of the seven appointed in chapter 6, was the first to preach the gospel in Samaria to the north of Jerusalem (8:1–25), and now the Lord was sending Philip to the south on another mission. This time the mission was to a person of a different nationality. Philip's divine appointment with the Ethiopian eunuch illustrates the way God uses people who are open to divine direction.

Philip Met an Ethiopian Official (Acts 8:26–27)

Now an angel of the Lord said to Philip, "Go south to the road—the desert road—that goes down from Jerusalem to Gaza." So he started out, and on his way he met an Ethiopian eunuch, an important official in charge of all the treasury of Candace, queen of the Ethiopians (vv. 26–27).

Philip was a humble and obedient servant of the Lord. He had preached in Samaria with great success. Then when Peter and John arrived, Philip was no longer in the spotlight as the main evangelist. However, that did not seem to bother him. He faded into the background until the Lord called him for another task. When that call came, Philip obeyed immediately—he headed south for the road to Gaza.

God's providence was at work. On the way, Philip met an **Ethiopian** who served as an official over the treasury of the queen mother. **Candace** was the traditional title given the queen mother, who was expected to perform official duties for the king, because the king was considered too sacred to engage in secular duties (*NIV Study Bible*). Through this man, Philip's message of the gospel could reach the Ethiopian court, and, in turn, the door to the Ethiopian populace would be opened to the gospel. Philip was attentive to God's leadership and was in the right place at the right time.

Ethiopia was probably the geographical area to the south of Egypt at the time of these events, though in Old Testament times the designation could vary from southern Egypt to parts of the Arabian Peninsula. Somehow this man had come in contact with the Jewish religion, had a scroll of the prophet Isaiah, and was reading it—probably in the Greek, Septuagint translation. Scrolls were expensive, and it was rare for individuals to possess such documents. It is likely that the official position of this man figured into his having such a prized document. Also, it is noteworthy that he must have been well educated to be able to read the Greek translation. His ability to read Greek also illustrates the reason why the New Testament was written in Greek—it was the way to reach the broadest possible audience in that day.

How this Ethiopian knew of the Jewish religion we do not know. But he must have been a proselyte to Judaism or a Gentile God-fearer who had accepted the Jewish faith. Certainly there were many such God-fearing Gentiles in Hellenistic areas where the apostle Paul later traveled. Apparently Jewish influence had also reached into Ethiopia.

Furthermore, this man was designated a **eunuch** (v. 27). This could simply mean he was a court official who was serving the queen, for many such officials were eunuchs. But it seems likely that he had indeed been mutilated. As such he would not be allowed to worship in the temple (Lev. 21:20; Deut. 23:1). It is true that Isaiah had predicted there would be a change in that command (56:3–5), and perhaps the strictures in Leviticus and Deuteronomy had been superseded. More likely, Jewish practice was probably not changed. Probably Isaiah was predicting the coming of the Christian church, where all such barriers have been removed. Given the evidence we have, it seems the Ethiopian was a eunuch and most likely a God-fearing Gentile rather than a proselyte.

WORDS FROM WESLEY

Acts 8:27

An eunuch—Chief officers were anciently called eunuchs, though not always literally such; because such used to be chief ministers in the eastern courts. (ENNT)

Philip Proclaimed the Gospel (Acts 8:27–35)

This man had gone to Jerusalem to worship, and on his way home was sitting in his chariot reading the book of Isaiah the prophet. The Spirit told Philip, "Go to that chariot and stay near it" (vv. 27–29).

The Ethiopian man's personal status related to Judaism may not be completely clear, but his devotion to the God of the Jews is obvious. He had traveled far to worship in Jerusalem. The journey must have been in the range of five hundred miles or even more. Furthermore, if he was a Gentile and a eunuch, his access to the temple was forbidden. Unless he was a proselyte and the Old Testament strictions had been removed, he could not enter the temple to worship. Nevertheless, he had journeyed to Jerusalem to worship, and now as he returned on the long journey home he was reading from the book of Isaiah. Philip was instructed to go near the chariot, and he heard the Ethiopian reading aloud. God's providence was at work, and Philip was ready to fulfill his role.

WORDS FROM WESLEY

Acts 8:28

Sitting in his chariot, he read the prophet Isaiah—God meeteth those that remember Him in his ways. It is good to read, hear, seek information even in a journey. Why should we not redeem all our time? (ENNT)

Then Philip ran up to the chariot and heard the man reading Isaiah the prophet. "Do you understand what you are reading?" Philip asked. "How can I," he said, "unless someone explains it to me?" So he invited Philip to come up and sit with him (vv. 30–31).

As the man read, Philip seized his opportunity and asked if he understood what he was reading. Learned Jewish rabbis have long debated the meaning of Isaiah 53, and this court official from another land was understandably puzzled by a passage that we understand to be speaking of Jesus and His sacrifice. The Ethiopian readily admitted he needed help in understanding what he was reading. Philip was available to help, and the man invited Philip to join him in the chariot.

WORDS FROM WESLEY

Acts 8:30

And Philip running to him, said, Understandest thou what thou readest—He did not begin about the weather, news, or the like. In speaking for God, we may frequently come to the point at once, without circumlocution. (ENNT)

The eunuch was reading this passage of Scripture: "He was led like a sheep to the slaughter, and as a lamb before the shearer is silent, so he did not open his mouth. In his humiliation he was deprived of justice. Who can speak of his descendants? For his life was taken from the earth." The eunuch asked Philip, "Tell me, please, who is the prophet talking about, himself or someone else?" (vv. 32–34).

Again we see God's providence in the passage the man was reading. There is surely no Old Testament prophecy that is more obviously predicting Jesus' sacrifice on our behalf. As the rabbis before him, the man wondered if Isaiah was speaking of **himself or someone else.** Some have suggested that the passage refers to the Jewish people and their suffering. As with many prophecies, only the fulfillment seen in Jesus' life and death had made the meaning clear to the apostles. Even when Jesus had explained what was going to happen to Him at Jerusalem, the apostles did not understand what He was talking about. But after Jesus' death and resurrection, the apostles began to understand. We can be sure Philip was aware of the Christian interpretation of the passage—that it was fulfilled in Jesus.

Then Philip began with that very passage of Scripture and told him the good news about Jesus (v. 35).

What a wonderful opening for Philip. Could anyone ask for a better opportunity to witness and explain **the good news**, the gospel? Like Jesus on the road to Emmaus (Luke 24:13–35), Philip began to explain **the good news about Jesus** (Acts 8:35), that Jesus had fulfilled this prophecy and the many other messianic prophecies of the Old Testament. God had prepared the Ethiopian's heart and mind, and God had brought Philip to the right place at the right time. The time was ripe for this man to enter the kingdom of God. He had already been so intrigued by the Jewish beliefs that he had traveled hundreds of miles by chariot to worship at Jerusalem. May we be tuned in to God's timing in people's lives as we meet them day by day.

The Baptism of the Ethiopian (Acts 8:36–40)

As they traveled along the road, they came to some water and the eunuch said, "Look, here is water. Why shouldn't I be baptized?" And he gave orders to stop the chariot. Then both Philip and the eunuch went down into the water and Philip baptized him (vv. 36–38).

How long did Philip talk with the eunuch? We do not know, but the man had grasped much of the gospel message and the process of becoming a believer, including baptism. No doubt water holes were rare in that desert region, and when they came to one, the man was ready. He wanted to accept the gospel Philip had explained. He was ready to put his faith in Jesus, the man who suffered and died as Isaiah had described in his prophecy.

Some manuscripts, such as those used in the New King James Version, add the words of verse 37: "Philip said, 'If you believe with all your heart, you may.' And he answered and said, 'I believe that Jesus Christ is the Son of God.'" Whether it was in Luke's original draft of Acts or not, this verse certainly seems to express what was in the eunuch's heart as he asked for and received baptism.

WORDS FROM WESLEY

Acts 8:36

And as they went on the way they came to a certain water—Thus, even the circumstances of the journey were under the direction of God. The kingdom of God suits itself to external circumstances, without any violence, as air yields to all bodies, and yet pervades all. (ENNT)

Was this baptism by immersion or not? The answer is a matter of interpretation. Maybe they happened upon a deep water hole along the desert road, but the likelihood is that it was a shallow pool and baptism was by sprinkling or effusion (pouring). However, we are told that Philip and the man did go down into the water and come up out of the water.

When should baptism be administered? Should it be immediately after a person expresses belief, as we see here, or sometime later? Certainly it was done immediately in several other cases in Acts (9:17–18; 10:47–48; 16:15; 16:33). Circumstances may dictate the answer. The early church soon required a waiting period for the new believer to be taught about the faith and to demonstrate sincerity. Today, a period of preparation for baptism often seems appropriate. However, circumstances may make immediate baptism necessary and appropriate. Certainly there is biblical precedence for baptism immediately after a person becomes a believer.

When they came up out of the water, the Spirit of the Lord suddenly took Philip away, and the eunuch did not see him again, but went on his way rejoicing. Philip, however, appeared at Azotus and traveled about, preaching the gospel in all the towns until he reached Caesarea (8:39–40).

With the baptism of the eunuch, Philip's assignment was done, and it sounds like the Spirit swept him away miraculously. The eunuch no longer had Philip as a resource, but he had experienced the good news Philip shared. Now he rejoiced. Philip's work was not done, however, and he appeared further north at **Azotus** and kept going **until he reached Caesarea**, which was on the coast some fifty miles north of Gaza. As he traveled through towns along the way, he preached the gospel. We are not told any details about later encounters he may have had, but we can be sure God was using him to reach others and to lead them to faith in Christ.

When persecution broke out after the martyrdom of Stephen, "the apostles were scattered throughout Judea and Samaria. . . . "Those who had been scattered preached the word wherever they went" (8:1, 4). We can be sure there were dozens of encounters more or less similar to Philip's that Luke did not record. Philip's encounters may have been more dramatic than most, but the work of spreading the gospel was being done wherever believers went. It is no wonder the early church grew rapidly. Today we serve the same God, who wants to use us to keep spreading the good news.

DISCUSSION

Although the gospel may be preached effectively to crowds, God saves souls one at a time. Sometimes He does so in regard to a highly unlikely person in a highly unlikely place.

1. Read Acts 8:26–29. What have you heard about Gaza in the news lately?

2. How does this passage show you that God cares about individuals?

3. Has the Lord directed you to share the gospel with someone of a different culture? If so, what were (or are) the circumstances?

4. How did the Scriptures prepare your heart to trust in Jesus as Savior?

5. Read Isaiah 53:3–7. How did Jesus fulfill the prophecies given in this passage?

6. Why do you agree or disagree that the Ethiopian eunuch had been in Jerusalem for Passover?

7. What passages would you most likely use to lead someone to Christ?

8. Why does joy often accompany baptism?

PRAYER

Father, help us to be sensitive to and aware of people who are searching for You. Please give us the wisdom and knowledge to answer their questions and concerns and draw them nearer to Your kingdom.

9

PARALYZED NO MORE

Acts 9:1–22

To be effectively used by God, we must let go of our past failures.

My husband is dying of throat cancer and needs the Lord," a woman confided in her pastor. However, when the pastor volunteered to visit the woman's husband, she replied, "I don't think he would let you enter the house. He hates preachers."

Not deterred by the warning, the pastor went to see the cancer patient. At first, the man was unwelcoming. He hardly looked at the pastor. But something about the pastor's demeanor and compassion broke down his resistance, and he opened his heart to receive Christ.

We must never write off even the most hardened sinner. This study underscores the fact that God can save even the "chief of sinners."

COMMENTARY

In chapters 1–8 of Acts, the major figure is the apostle Peter. Then, beginning in chapter 9 Luke focused on the other major figure, Saul, the Jewish zealot later called Paul. Luke was not through with his account of Peter, however, for Peter appears as the lead figure in Acts 9:32–43 and in chapters 10–12. A brief account of Peter's testimony at the Council of Jerusalem is given in chapter 15, but Saul/Paul is the dominant figure from Acts 13 on.

In Acts 9:1–22, we read of the miraculous transformation of Saul from persecutor of the church to leading apologist and evangelist for the church. The dramatic change in Saul, along with his powerful apology for the way of Jesus, led to extreme opposition from traditional Jews. Twice in chapter 9 Jews plotted to kill Saul (9:23, 29). In fact, to save his life, the brothers at Jerusalem "took him down to Caesarea and sent him off to Tarsus" (9:30). As Saul had been zealous for Judaism, he now was equally zealous for Christ. No wonder God used special means to turn this sincere, hard-driving leader from his Jewish ways to effective Christian missionary. In fact, when the disciples at Antioch were the first to be called "Christian," Saul was among them.

What a change was evident in Saul's life after he met Jesus on the road to Damascus. What might God be able to do through similar dramatic changes in the lives of other sincere, devoted religious leaders among Muslims, Hindus, Buddhists, Jews, and others? God is still in the business of changing lives. Pray that there may be many Damascus-road experiences in our time.

Paul's Damascus Road Conversion (Acts 9:1–9)

Meanwhile, Saul was still breathing out murderous threats against the Lord's disciples. He went to the high priest and asked him for letters to the synagogues in Damascus (vv. 1–2).

Saul was determined to put an end to **the Way** (v. 2), which he considered a heretical movement. Persecution had scattered the disciples throughout Judea and Samaria, and some disciples had fled all the way to Damascus of Syria 150 miles north of Jerusalem. Saul wanted to stamp out this sect before it brought any more damage to his beloved Jewish faith. He asked for letters authorizing him to search for disciples **in Damascus, so that if he found any there who belonged to the Way, whether men or women, he might take them as prisoners to Jerusalem. As he neared Damascus on his journey, suddenly a light from heaven flashed around him. He fell to the ground and heard a voice say to him, "Saul, Saul, why do you persecute me?"** (vv. 2–4).

Saul's world was turned upside down when he saw the light and heard the voice of Jesus. The young educated Pharisee was shaken out of his certainty; he was no longer in control. He was so frightened that **he fell to the ground** (v. 4).

WORDS FROM WESLEY

Acts 9:3

And suddenly—When God suddenly and vehemently attacks a sinner, it is the highest act of mercy. (ENNT)

"Who are you, Lord?" Saul asked. "I am Jesus, whom you are persecuting," he replied. "Now get up and go into the city, and you will be told what you must do" (vv. 5–6).

Did Saul have any idea it was Jesus' voice he was hearing? Probably not until he was told. But surely the death of Stephen a few months earlier had impressed him. He had probably pondered Stephen's sermon (Acts 7) and the events surrounding the trial and stoning. Now was his moment of truth as he saw the light from heaven and heard the voice of Jesus in a manner similar to Stephen's vision (7:56). **The men traveling with Saul stood there speechless; they heard the sound but did not see anyone** (9:7). Surely they, too, were frightened—their leader had fallen to the ground in fright, and they heard him speaking to someone they could not see.

WORDS FROM WESLEY

Acts 9:6

It shall be told thee—So God himself sends Saul to be taught by a man, as the angel does Cornelius, ch. 10:5. Admirable condescension! That the Lord deals with us by men, like ourselves. (ENNT)

Saul got up from the ground, but when he opened his eyes he could see nothing. So they led him by the hand into Damascus. For three days he was blind, and did not eat or drink anything (vv. 8–9).

Saul, who was accustomed to being in control, was now blind and helpless. The blindness gave him time to ponder what had happened. **For three days he . . . did not eat or drink** (v. 9). During that time he must have thought about the events related to Stephen's death and the persecution of believers he had instigated—and the voice of Jesus: **"Why do you persecute me?"** (v. 4). Saul may have been overwhelmed by guilt after hearing the voice of Jesus. But mostly he was probably confused.

WORDS FROM WESLEY

Acts 9:9

And he was three days—An important season! So long he seems to have been in the pangs of the new birth. *Without sight*—By scales growing over his eyes, to intimate to him the blindness of the state he had been in, to impress him with a deeper sense of the almighty power of Christ, and to turn his thoughts inward, while he was less capable of conversing with outward objects. This was likewise a manifest token to others, of what had happened to him in his journey, and ought to have humbled and convinced those bigoted Jews, to whom he had been sent from the Sanhedrim. (ENNT)

Ananias Ministered to Saul (Acts 9:10–19)

In Damascus there was a disciple named Ananias. The Lord called to him in a vision, "Ananias!" "Yes, Lord," he answered. The Lord told him, "Go to the house of Judas on Straight Street and ask for a man from Tarsus named Saul, for he is praying. In a vision he has seen a man named Ananias come and place his hands on him to restore his sight" (vv. 10–12).

From this passage we learn Saul had been praying, and the Lord had given him a vision to encourage him and give him hope while he was blind. We also learn of a disciple in Damascus: **Ananias**. Furthermore, we learn this man was attuned to the voice of the Lord, judging from the conversation between the Lord and him. Ananias was given specific directions to follow: **house of Judas, Straight Street, Saul**. Also, Ananias was told Saul was expecting him because of the vision Saul had been given. Why does God sometimes use miraculous events to effect an individual's conversion? God is sovereign and works as He pleases. Our task is to pray and obey.

"Lord," Ananias answered, "I have heard many reports about this man and all the harm he has done to your saints in Jerusalem. And he has come here with authority from the chief priests to arrest all who call on your name" (vv. 13–14).

Saul's reputation had preceded him to Damascus. Ananias knew about Saul's persecution in Jerusalem and about his official mission to extend the persecution to Damascus. The Lord's words of commission to Ananias were alarming. He'd hoped to avoid Saul, not confront him. This was not a task Ananias desired, and he told the Lord his misgivings.

But the Lord said to Ananias, "Go! This man is my chosen instrument to carry my name before the Gentiles and their kings and before the people of Israel. I will show him how much he must suffer for my name" (vv. 15–16).

The Lord answered Ananias's doubts with insight into Saul's future mission. Saul would be the Lord's **chosen instrument** and would **suffer** much for Jesus' name. In his vision, Ananias had been informed that Saul was blind (for Ananias was to lay hands on Saul to restore his sight [v. 12]). Despite his fear, Ananias was reassured through the Lord's words.

Had the Lord revealed his plan for Saul's life to Saul before this? In Luke's account, we learn of the future mission of Saul to the Gentiles from the revelation to Ananias. It seems Ananias had the privilege of revealing God's plan to Saul (22:14).

WORDS FROM WESLEY

Acts 9:15

He is a chosen vessel to bear my name —That is, to testify of me. It is undeniable, that some men are unconditionally chosen or elected, to do some works for God. (ENNT)

Then Ananias went to the house and entered it. Placing his hands on Saul, he said, "Brother Saul, the Lord—Jesus, who appeared to you on the road as you were coming here—has sent me so that you may see again and be filled with the Holy Spirit" (9:17).

WORDS FROM WESLEY

Acts 9:17

The Lord hath sent me —Ananias does not tell Saul all which Christ had said concerning him. It was not expedient that he should know yet to how great a dignity he was called. (ENNT)

Perhaps Ananias was still frightened as he obediently went to find Saul. If so, his words—calling him **brother**—do not reveal fear, but kindness and love for this former persecutor. He laid his hands on Saul and **immediately, something like scales fell from Saul's eyes, and he could see again** (v. 18). In short order, Saul regained his sight, was filled with the Spirit, and was baptized. Then **after taking some food, he regained his strength** (v. 19). Saul had been without food or drink for three days and was in need of refreshment. Though we do not hear of Ananias again other than in Paul's testimony (22:12), this faithful servant played a critical role in God's plans for the apostle Paul.

Paul's Initial Ministry (Acts 9:19–22)

Saul spent several days with the disciples in Damascus. At once he began to preach in the synagogues that Jesus is the Son of God (vv. 19–20).

Saul wasted no time on regrets. He heard the voice of Jesus; he prayed and thought for three days; and the vision of Ananias had come true. Now he was ready for this new mission. Soon he was proclaiming Jesus as the Son of God openly in the synagogues. A dramatic turnaround—from persecutor to proclaimer.

Galatians tells us that Paul went to Arabia during this period for several months, possibly as long as two or three years. There he received revelations about Jesus, and there he formulated his gospel based on those revelations (Gal. 1:11–17). We do not know why Luke gave no account of this trip to Arabia. Did this time in Arabia occur before Saul started preaching in Damascus? Acts leads us to believe he was preaching almost immediately. How to fit the visit to Arabia into the Acts account is a puzzle for biblical scholars. Acts 9:23 does speak of "many days." Certainly the Galatians passage makes it clear more was happening in the early church than Luke recorded in Acts.

All those who heard him were astonished and asked, "Isn't he the man who raised havoc in Jerusalem among those who call on this name? And hasn't he come here to take them as prisoners to the chief priests?" Yet Saul grew more and more powerful and baffled the Jews living in Damascus by proving that Jesus is the Christ (vv. 21–22).

Saul's about-face amazed the Jews living in Damascus. They wondered what had happened to change his message. He was now supporting the cause he had set out to attack. He even had official authorization from the chief priests. As time passed, Saul's apologetic ability grew, and he proved from Scripture that Jesus was the promised Messiah (Christ). Saul's past had brought grief to believers, but his future was growing brighter day by day. Saul started on a new path that he kept following until his death some thirty years later.

In Paul's last letter we read these triumphant words: "I have fought the good fight, I have finished the race, I have kept the faith. Now there is in store for me the crown of righteousness, which the Lord, the righteous Judge, will award to me on that day—and not only to me, but also to all who have longed for his appearing" (2 Tim. 4:7–8). May we be among those "who have longed for his appearing."

DISCUSSION

Is anyone beyond God's power to save? Can even the most vehement enemy of Christianity become a believer? The conversion of Saul of Tarsus shows that nothing is too hard for God.

1. Why is "the Way" (Acts 9:2) a good designation for believers in Jesus?

2. How do you explain the fact that such a religious person as Saul could make "murderous threats" against believers? How is similar aggression carried out today?

3. How had Saul been persecuting Jesus?

4. Read Acts 9:7. Without using the word *speechless*, how would you describe Saul's traveling companions' reaction to what happened on the road to Damascus?

5. Why do you suppose the Lord blinded Saul for three days?

6. Why, do you think, did Saul not eat or drink anything for those three days?

7. Read Acts 9:10–16. How did the Lord remove Ananias's reluctance to visit Saul?

8. The Lord changed Saul's life dramatically. How has He changed your life?

PRAYER

Father, open our eyes that we may see people as You do and not define them by their past. Show us how we can be used in the lives of others to bring transformation to them and to the kingdom.

10

GOD DOES NOT SHOW FAVORITISM

Acts 10:1–20

God invites all to participate in His kingdom.

Have you known people who visit a restaurant but make a big fuss if they think the food seems slightly under- or overcooked? Some picky eaters complain if they see a trace of dishwasher residue on a fork, knife, or plate. They may cause quite a scene if they see a few crumbs on their table or chairs.

The apostle Peter must not have been a picky eater. After all, he must have encountered a few fish bones in his life. But when God offered him food that wasn't "kosher," he refused to eat it. The occasion became a learning experience in which Peter learned about God's love for Gentiles.

Let this study deepen your love for all people.

COMMENTARY

Cornelius and Peter could not have been more different. Cornelius was a Roman centurion, a leader in command of one hundred soldiers, living in a beautiful city that eventually became the center of government for Palestine. He had great influence not only on his family and soldiers, but also on his area of an entire city. Peter, in contrast, was a Jew with little worldly education, a rough man who used to labor among nets and fish, hardened by winds and sea air. He was in command only on his fishing boat.

Yet the power of God was at work in both these men's lives, transforming their thinking. Although Cornelius was a Gentile, he is described as a God-fearer, someone not yet converted to

Judaism, but following its monotheistic (one god) belief system rather than the religion of his culture. Likewise, Peter, a devout Jew, had his life and religious ideas turned upside down by his teacher, Jesus. His views of God's kingdom had been transformed by the life, teaching, and death of the one he pronounced "Messiah," Savior of the Jewish people. Peter was most comfortable with other fishermen, yet God kept expanding his horizon, changing him into a leader He could use anywhere, anytime.

God had been preparing both men for an encounter that would have far-reaching spiritual and religious implications. Cornelius needed to find out about Jesus Christ, while Peter needed to know to whom he should reach out in ministry. The journeys Peter and Cornelius had begun separately would, through the call of God and their obedience, intersect in a historic meeting that would not only change their lives, but transform the thinking of the new Christian church. As a result, Christianity became not just a reform movement within Judaism, but a new religion with Jesus Christ as its center, welcoming Jews and Gentiles alike.

The Obedience of Cornelius (Acts 10:1–8)

Cornelius was clearly a man of character. Roman centurions were soldiers carefully selected for their leadership, obedience, and noble qualities. Additionally, Cornelius was seriously seeking God. Although not a convert to Judaism (since he is called **God-fearing** [v. 2], not a *proselyte*, one who has been circumcised), he was emulating Jewish religious ways. Apparently, he was accustomed to praying regularly and at the usual times of prayer, such as at the hour of evening incense, **three in the afternoon** (v. 3). In addition to his healthy prayer life, Cornelius was a generous benefactor, another duty of a **devout** Jew (v. 2). He was serious enough about his responsibilities to God and people that all the Jews in Caesarea had great respect for him (10:22), a compliment, considering the Jewish opinion of Roman occupation. God chose to reward him for his diligence (v. 4).

WORDS FROM WESLEY

Acts 10:1

And there was a certain man—The first-fruits of the *Gentiles, in Cesarea*—Where Philip had been before (ch. 8:40). So that the doctrine of salvation by faith in Jesus was not unknown there. Cesarea was the seat of the civil government, as Jerusalem was of the ecclesiastical. It is observable, that the Gospel made its way first through the metropolitan cities. So it first seized Jerusalem and Cesarea: afterward *Philippi, Athens, Corinth, Ephesus, Rome* itself. (ENNT)

When a person is sincerely seeking God, God will help him or her. As Hebrews 11:6 states, "Without faith it is impossible to please God, because anyone who comes to him must believe that he exists and that he rewards those who earnestly seek him." This was seen in Cornelius, who was being obedient to what he knew of God through his observation of the Jews in Caesarea. He would have observed the difficulty of the devout Jews in meeting the requirements of the Mosaic law, yet he hungered for God enough to imitate their holy practices. His duties as a Roman soldier would have made it difficult for him to fully convert to Judaism, because he would not have been able to obey many of the time-bound commands, such as going to the temple at specific seasons. Cornelius still chose to follow God as an outsider peeking in the window and imitating what he saw. However, he would soon discover he was not required to observe Jewish Law to come into the kingdom of God. His obedience was rewarded with a gift beyond his imagination: He would be part of the *new* covenant with God.

WORDS FROM WESLEY

Acts 10:4

Thus, we may observe, the men of God, in ancient times, always joined prayer and fasting together . . . ; it remains only, in order to our observing such a fast as is acceptable to the Lord, that we add alms thereto; works of mercy, after our power, both to the bodies and souls of men: "With such sacrifices" also "God is well pleased." Thus the angel declares to Cornelius, fasting and praying in his house, "Thy prayers and thine alms are come up for a memorial before God" (Acts 10:4, &c). (WJW, vol. 14, 360)

Because of this obedience to spiritual discipline, Cornelius was primed and ready when God called. Cornelius did not question the angel, although he must have been curious. Who was this man named Simon Peter? Why did he need to meet with him? In what way would this visit be a reward for his devotion? And what was this Jew doing at the house of a tanner, a man who cured animal skins and was often avoided because of his smelly occupation? A soldier alert for the command of his superior, Cornelius recognized the order and acted upon it: **When the angel who spoke to him had gone, Cornelius called two of his servants and a devout soldier who was one of his attendants. He told them everything that had happened and sent them to Joppa** (Acts 10:7–8).

Finally, Cornelius was a positive influence on those around him: **He and all his family were devout and God-fearing** (v. 2). His household and the men under his authority were affected by his devotion to God (v. 7). He was a witness of God for his family, servants, and soldiers, revealing his true spirituality and leadership ability. He was not embarrassed to tell his servants of this supernatural vision, but told them everything that had happened, something not required of a centurion who was accustomed to having his orders obeyed without question (v. 8).

The Obedience of Peter (Acts 10:9–20)

Peter also was a praying man, a devout Jew (v. 9). He was sincerely devoted to Jesus Christ, the one he recognized as the Messiah of the Jewish people. But the commands of his Lord and the demands of his religion were heading for a collision.

Peter had a more difficult task than Cornelius in determining his response to God's call. Instead of the hope offered in the vision of Cornelius, Peter's vision was disgusting to a devout Jew. The sheet he saw **contained all kinds of four-footed animals, as well as reptiles of the earth and birds of the air** (v. 12). He was commanded to eat these animals, some of which were unclean, forbidden for Jews according to Leviticus 11. Peter was horrified: **"Surely not, Lord!" Peter replied. "I have never eaten anything impure or unclean"** (v. 14). Yet the vision, and thus the command, was given three times. There was no mistaking God meant what God said.

WORDS FROM WESLEY

Acts 10:14

But Peter said, in nowise, Lord—When God commands a strange or seemingly improper thing, the first objection frequently finds pardon. But it ought not to be repeated. This doubt and delay of St. Peter had several good effects. Hereby the will of God in this important point, was made more evident and incontestable. And Peter also, having been so slow of belief himself, could the more easily bear the doubting of his brethren, ch. 11:2, &c. (ENNT)

But while Peter was still wondering what this vision meant, the call came from the Holy Spirit: **"Simon, three men are looking for you. So get up and go downstairs. Do not hesitate to go with them, for I have sent them"** (vv. 19–20). Peter obeyed, no questions asked. Already he had an idea of what he was being asked to do.

Peter's progress on this journey toward God's vision is evident in the fact that he was staying at the house of a man who worked with dead animal skins, something Jews considered unclean. Scripture does not record how and why he came to be staying with Simon the tanner. However, clearly God had already begun preparing him for a shift in thinking. Not only did Peter seek these Gentile men according to the prompting of the Spirit, but he asked them into Simon's house as guests (v. 23). Peter's obedience was remarkable for several reasons.

WORDS FROM WESLEY

Acts 10:17

While Peter doubted in himself, behold the men—Frequently the things which befall us *within* and from *without* at the same time, are a key to each other. The things which thus concur and agree together, ought to be diligently attended to. (ENNT)

First, Jews did not interact socially with Gentiles. Peter made this clear when he arrived at Cornelius's house and went inside, a fact specifically mentioned by Luke (v. 25). Peter explained to the group of friends and relatives, "You are well aware that it is against our law for a Jew to associate with a Gentile or visit him. But God has shown me that I should not call any man impure or unclean" (v. 28). Peter had realized the vision didn't have to do with food, but with relationships. God was continuing to adjust his vision. Amazingly, God cared about the Gentiles as well as the Jews, a concept that was foreign to the thinking of most Jews, who rejoiced in their status as God's chosen people.

How was Peter able to understand the meaning of the vision? He realized God's timing was significant. God had spoken to Cornelius, who had sent his servants on their way so they would arrive at the right time, when Peter had just received his vision (v. 19). Joppa was thirty miles south of Caesarea, so it took them about a day to get there (v. 9). Peter could see God had prepared the person to whom he was to speak, just as God had prepared him so he could respond.

A second reason Peter's response was remarkable is because of his history of mistakes. Peter had an impulsive nature. Often his instant loving reactions must have warmed Jesus' heart. Unfortunately, he had a difficult time adjusting his thinking, based on his religious upbringing, to the new vision of the kingdom of God Jesus taught. Peter's impulsivity frequently disappointed Jesus. Jesus had to keep patiently explaining, "No, Peter, you haven't got it yet." Can you imagine how difficult this vision was for Peter to act on after his repeated failures and misunderstandings of Jesus' teaching?

However, Peter was determined to obey God. This resolve is evident earlier in the book of Acts in his and John's response to the Sanhedrin when they were told they could no longer preach in Jesus' name: "Judge for yourselves whether it is right in God's sight to obey you rather than God. For we cannot help speaking about what we have seen and heard" (4:19–20).

So Peter preached the gospel to a *Gentile* audience, one gathered by a soldier in the *Roman* army, an iron force that had subjugated his people. Peter's faith in acting on the command of God was rewarded when "the Holy Spirit came on all who heard the message" of Jesus Christ as Son of God (10:44). The group of circumcised believers who accompanied Peter was amazed "that the gift of the Holy Spirit had been poured out even on the Gentiles" (v. 45), evident by the fact that they were speaking in tongues. News of this event spread all over Judea, and Peter had to go to Jerusalem to explain what he had done to his appalled Jewish Christian brothers (11:1–3). After he explained what had happened, they recognized God was using their brother Peter to broaden their vision of the kingdom of God (11:18).

During His time on earth, Jesus had broken down walls between ethnic groups in His ministry. Peter's vision was a command that the church was to *continue* breaking down walls, this time between Jew and Gentile. Jesus had commanded this ministry before He returned to heaven (1:8), and now, through the Holy Spirit, He provided further instructions. Thank God for the command that Gentiles be included. Thank God a powerful individual like Cornelius was willing to talk to a simple Jewish fisherman. Thank God Peter was obedient to the command of God and stepped out of his religious box.

We must continue to look for God's vision of the kingdom and not remain constrained by our traditional ideas. We must continually examine our ministries and decide if Jesus is asking us to change our ways to reach the world for Him. Most of all, we must be obedient to the command of God on our lives, as Cornelius and Peter were.

DISCUSSION

Some old attitudes die hard, don't they? We may avoid certain people because they are culturally different. We may judge a person's character by the way he or she dresses. But there is no partiality with God.

1. How does it encourage you to know that God arranged for Cornelius to hear the gospel?

2. How do you feel about unbelievers who earnestly pray and seek God?

3. What word best summarizes Cornelius's character? Why that word?

4. Read Acts 10:9–16. Why do you agree or disagree that Peter's reaction to God's command to "kill and eat" indicates spiritual pride on his part?

5. Read 1 Timothy 4:1–3. Based on this passage, are Christians free to eat food the Levitical law banned? Why or why not?

6. Read Acts 10:17–25. What did it take to get Peter to the home of Cornelius?

7. How has God patiently worked in your life to get you to obey Him?

8. Why do you agree or disagree that most believers are reluctant to move out of their comfort zones to share the gospel?

PRAYER

Father, make us sensitive to Your Spirit that we may know Your will, even when it surprises us. And help us be willing to take risks and go out of our way to serve You.

DON'T STOP NOW

Acts 12:25; 13:5; 15:36–39

Our mistakes and failures do not limit God's ability to
effectively use us for His glory.

$\mathbf{A}$nyone who thinks teaching is a cushy job hasn't tried it. Education majors find out during their student teaching assignments that the profession can be physically, mentally, and emotionally grueling. Although student teachers work and learn alongside experienced teachers, some decide that teaching is not for them and then give up.

John Mark toiled alongside two outstanding missionaries, Barnabas and Paul, but he abandoned missions at least for a while. Later, Barnabas wanted to take Mark on another missionary journey, but Paul refused. Nevertheless, eventually Paul forgave Mark and considered him a valuable asset.

This study emphasizes the importance of practicing forgiveness and reconciliation instead of giving up on a fellow believer.

COMMENTARY

The book of Acts revolves around towering figures from the New Testament period—Peter in Acts 1–12 and Paul in Acts 13–28. It introduces us to significant leaders such as Stephen, Philip, and Barnabas. But scattered through its verses are bits and pieces of information about other early Christians. One such person is John Mark. Piecing together these hints from Acts and from early church history tells a fascinating story of a young man who had a great opportunity early on, fell flat on his face with it, got up, and, under the patient ministry of the Holy Spirit, left a rich spiritual legacy for all Christian generations. John was his Jewish name; Mark was his Gentile name. *John* means Jehovah is gracious, and as we shall see, the Lord was gracious to John Mark.

The first mention of John Mark is almost certainly in the gospel of Mark. The event took place in the garden of Gethsemane on the night before Jesus was crucified. The officers had arrived with Judas to arrest Jesus. "A young man, wearing nothing but a linen garment, was following Jesus. When they seized him, he fled naked, leaving his garment behind" (Mark 14:51–52). It seems to have been the custom of authors at that time not to mention themselves by name (John 21:24). This passage has nothing to do with what comes before or what follows. It appears to be the vivid memory of a frightening, embarrassing incident early in the life of John Mark, the author of the second gospel.

We do know the name of Mark's mother: Mary. Apparently his father was dead. Their home in Jerusalem is referred to as Mary's house. She was well-to-do, as the house was large enough to house a Christian congregation, and she had at least one servant girl (Acts 12:12–13). We also know John Mark was a cousin of Barnabas (Col. 4:10). Barnabas was a Levite from Cyprus and a landowner (Acts 4:36–37). Both of these aspects of his background indicate that John Mark came from a comfortable economic situation. The only other hint of John Mark's early life is found in 1 Peter 5:13, in which Peter called him his "son." This probably means "spiritual son" in the same way Paul referred to Timothy (1 Tim. 1:2), and has led some to believe Peter had led John Mark to Christ. Peter was acquainted with Mary's house in Jerusalem (Acts 12:12–17).

Mark's Great Opportunity (Acts 12:25; 13:5)

Mark's first opportunity to serve the early church (that we know of) comes when Barnabas and Saul (Paul) came to Jerusalem, bringing a special offering from their church in Antioch for the needy Christians. When they had presented the offering and completed their visit, they returned to Antioch, **taking with them John, also called Mark** (12:25).

WORDS FROM WESLEY

Acts 12:25

Saul returned—To Antioch; *taking John surnamed Mark*—The son of Mary (at whose house the disciples met, to pray for Peter), who was sister to Barnabas. (ENNT)

Once back in Antioch, Mark found himself immersed in the most exciting, dynamic church of that day. Jews and Gentiles had the walls between them broken down by the gospel. They were eating together, worshiping together, fellowshipping together. The church was growing rapidly. It was an innovative congregation. The people of Antioch had begun to call the members Christians.

The three men had been in Antioch apparently for a short time when the pastoral staff had a prayer and fasting retreat (Acts 13:1–3). In that meeting, the Holy Spirit laid it on the hearts of the pastors to separate Barnabas and Saul for a special work to which He was calling them. They continued in prayer and fasting until the Spirit's leadership was fully confirmed. Then they laid hands on them and sent them off.

Acts 13:4–5 tells us they were sent on their way by the Holy Spirit and that **John** Mark **was with them as their helper** (13:5). Some Bible scholars think this describes Mark as roughly equivalent to a modern-day business manager serving a traveling band or sports team. The term refers to an official assistant, not a slave. Luke spoke of servants (same word as **helper**) of the word, referring to those who wrote the events of the gospel (Acts 1:2). And the historian Papias spoke of Mark as taking notes from the preaching of Peter later in Mark's life (*Zondervan Pictorial Encyclopedia of the Bible*). So Mark was probably more than a baggage carrier or errand boy.

Mark had no way of knowing what we know—that the Holy Spirit had given him an opportunity to be in on the beginning of a worldwide missionary endeavor that would plant churches in Asia Minor, later in Europe, and in our own generation reaching to the uttermost parts of the earth. He accompanied Barnabas and Saul in their ministry on Cyprus. Saul (Paul) became the main spokesman on Cyprus and had a dramatic encounter with a false prophet, who was left temporarily blind as a result. By the time they left there, "Barnabas and Saul" had become "Paul and his companions" (Acts 13:13). Some Bible scholars have assumed Mark resented the obvious shift of leadership from his cousin to Paul. Some say he may have been intimidated by the two older men and felt he would not be missed. Still others have suggested that since John Mark came from a comfortable home, the rigors of travel were not to his liking. We do not know why it happened, but John Mark left them at Perga in Pamphylia and returned to Jerusalem, his home.

WORDS FROM WESLEY

Acts 13:13

John withdrawing from them returned—Tired with the fatigue, or shrinking from danger. (ENNT)

Mark's Second Chance (Acts 15:36–39)

John Mark failed his great opportunity. But God was not through with him. Paul and Barnabas continued on the first missionary journey, returning to Antioch, where "they gathered the church together and reported all that God had done through them and how he had opened the door of faith to the Gentiles. And they stayed there [in Antioch] a long time" (Acts 14:27–28).

Then some men from Jerusalem came to Antioch, saying the Gentiles must observe the Mosaic law to be saved. Paul and Barnabas took an appeal concerning this to the church leaders, and in the great council of Jerusalem, the church decided only a few things would be asked of the Gentiles: "Abstain from food sacrificed to idols, from blood, from the meat of strangled animals and from sexual immorality" (15:29). Then Paul and Barnabas, along with two other men, Silas and Judas, were sent back to Antioch to carry the good news.

It is not clear whether Mark accompanied Barnabas on the trip back from Jerusalem. But by the time this study picks up the story, he was back in Antioch. Paul proposed to Barnabas a second journey to **go back and visit the brothers in all the towns where** they **preached the word of the Lord and see how they** were **doing** (v. 36).

WORDS FROM WESLEY

Acts 15:36

Let us go and visit the brethren in every city where we have preached—This was all that St. Paul designed at first. But it was not all that God designed by his journey, whose providence carried him much farther than he intended. *And see how they do*—How their souls prosper: how they grow in faith, hope, love: what else ought to be the grand and constant inquiry in every ecclesiastical visitation? Reader, How dost thou do? (ENNT)

Barnabas agreed and proposed that they take **John, also called Mark, with them, but Paul did not think it wise to take him, because he had deserted them in Pamphylia and had**

not continued with them in the work (vv. 37–38). This led to **a sharp disagreement** (v. 39). One thing about the Scriptures. They never present their heroes in anything but an honest picture—faults as well as virtues. The Greek word for **sharp disagreement** refers to irritation. It is the source of our English word *paroxysm*, which can mean a sudden outburst. The verb form of this word was used by Paul when he wrote in the great love chapter that love "is not easily angered" (1 Cor. 13:5). Neither man would yield. They broke up the partnership and went their separate ways. Even the most mature saints can have blind spots that hinder relationships. And as we will see, this is not the end of the story.

WORDS FROM WESLEY

Acts 15:38

But Paul thought it not right—To trust him again, who had deserted them before: who had shrunk from the labour and danger of converting those they were now going to confirm. (ENNT)

One would hesitate to suggest that the Holy Spirit prompted this disagreement. In fact, at first it may have seemed a tragedy. But God uses our mistakes for His glory. The result of this sharp disagreement was the multiplication of missionary parties, and a second chance for John Mark. **Barnabas took Mark and sailed for Cyprus** (Acts 15:39)—back to where John Mark had accompanied them on the first journey. Paul took Silas and headed in a different direction (15:40–41). We know Paul and Silas went on to found churches in Europe. We don't have the details on Barnabas and Mark's ministry. But it is evident that Mark made the most of his second and subsequent opportunities.

Paul had adamantly refused to allow Mark to go with them on the second missionary journey. But Paul could accept evidence that he was wrong. He mentioned John Mark three times in his letters—all favorably. The letters to the Colossians and Philemon may have been carried by the same messenger from Rome to Asia Minor. In Colossians 4:10, Mark was with Paul, and Paul included greetings to the church at Colosse from "Mark, the cousin of Barnabas." In Philemon 23–24, again Paul included Mark among those sending greetings and also among those he called "my fellow workers."

The strongest evidence of Barnabas's good judgment and Paul's change of heart is found when Paul told Timothy, "Get Mark and bring him with you, because he is helpful to me in my ministry" (2 Tim. 4:11). By this time, Paul was in prison in Rome for the final time, with his execution approaching (4:6–8). Both Mark and Paul had long since left their differences behind as both served the Lord effectively.

Mark's opportunities and ministry were not over yet. In 1 Peter 5:13, Peter included greetings from "my son Mark." Papias, a bishop in Asia Minor, who served about fifty to sixty years after Paul's death, as well as other writers of that period, spoke of Mark as having interpreted for Peter in Rome and having written our second gospel. It is widely believed by scholars to have been in a real sense Peter's gospel that Mark put down with pen and ink. It is the shortest, fastest-moving, and most vivid of the four gospels and is a priceless treasure that Mark left for succeeding generations of Christians. Tradition says he established churches in Alexandria, Egypt, and that he was buried in Venice, Italy. Thank God John Mark had a second chance. And let us realize that God will not drop us either because of a single or repeated blunders.

DISCUSSION

Has God ever given up on you? Have you ever given up on a fellow Christian? Because God can turn disappointments into His appointments, we should never give up on anyone, including ourselves.

1. How would you describe John Mark's family background?

2. How might parents encourage a son or daughter to serve the Lord?

3. Read Acts 12:25. Why do you agree or disagree that Saul and Barnabas exerted a strong, positive influence of John Mark?

4. How have one or two Christians contributed greatly to your spiritual development?

5. How do you think John Mark assisted Barnabas and Saul?

6. Read Acts 13:13. What do you think prompted John Mark to leave the mission field and return to Jerusalem?

7. Read Acts 15:36–39.Why do you agree or disagree that Paul held a grudge against Mark?

8. Read 2 Timothy 4:11. How do you know Paul eventually forgave Mark and was reconciled to him?

9. Why do you agree or disagree that it is better to try to serve the Lord and quit temporarily than not to try at all?

PRAYER

Father, thank You that You are a God who gives second chances, even when we sometimes fail at the awesome opportunities You give us. Help us to show the same grace to others.

FAITHFUL STUDENTS

Acts 18:18–28

The church functions best when believers willingly
share their understanding with others.

A pastor observed that his church was full of willing workers. "A few are willing to work, and the rest are willing to let them work," he explained.

Another pastor complained, "When we need to move the piano from one side of the sanctuary to the other, many people volunteer to carry the bench, but no one volunteers to help lift the piano."

Fortunately, most churches are composed of people who want to help wherever they are needed. Those people resemble Priscilla and Aquila, who opened their home for worship and mentored Apollos.

This study will strengthen your desire to serve others out of love for Jesus.

COMMENTARY

The New Testament paints a wonderful picture of how Christians need each other. It uses the metaphor of a body (1 Cor. 12:12–31). One is a hand, another is a foot, and neither can say of the other that it is not needed. The whole body must work together. We need each other. The New Testament also uses the metaphor of a temple. It says that we are "built on the foundation of the apostles and prophets, with Christ Jesus himself as the chief cornerstone. In him the whole building is joined together and rises to become a holy temple in the Lord. And in him you too are being built together to become a dwelling in which God lives by his Spirit" (Eph. 2:20–22). We need each other. Together we become the dwelling place of God.

The Christian life was meant to be lived in communion with other followers of Christ. While we must individually receive Jesus into our lives, we must communally live out the life of Christ in us. "Lone Ranger" Christians are non-biblical Christians. This New Testament picture of how Christians need each other is the big picture. Often though, Christians have trouble working out the details. How should we be involved in each other's lives? What does it mean to be part of the same body or temple? The story of Aquila and Priscilla helps us with some of these details. They show what it means to be practically involved in someone's life.

Established in Ephesus (Acts 18:18–23)

Aquila and his wife, Priscilla, were Jewish. Aquila had grown up in Pontus (modern-day northern Turkey), which bordered Galatia. First Peter was written to the churches in this area. There were people from Pontus who were present on the day of Pentecost. They heard the believers speak the gospel and praise God in their own language. People from Pontus were some of the first believers.

The Bible does not say where Priscilla was from. Nor does it tell how Priscilla and Aquila came to know the Lord. Maybe it was through the testimony of one of those early believers. They might have come to know Christ through Paul.

What we do know is that because of an edict from the Roman emperor Claudius, all Jewish people were expelled from Rome. Living in Rome at the time of the edict, Aquila and Priscilla were expelled and moved to Corinth.

As tentmakers, they plied their trade in Corinth. When Paul moved to Corinth, there was a natural affinity with the couple, because he also was a tentmaker. Paul moved into Aquila and Priscilla's house and worked with them.

Paul went to the synagogue every Sabbath and tried to persuade people that Jesus was the Messiah. Priscilla and Aquila would have been part of that synagogue. It is not hard to imagine that Paul significantly influenced the people he lived with. When Timothy and Silas arrived in Corinth, Paul quit making tents so he could preach full time. Among the many events of Paul's eighteen months in Corinth was Priscilla and Aquila becoming established (or more established) in the faith.

When the time came for Paul to move on from Corinth to Ephesus, he took Aquila and Priscilla with him. Paul stayed a short time, but the couple made Ephesus their place of residence. Aquila and Priscilla are the only couple in the New Testament who we are explicitly told were involved in ministry together. Paul called them "fellow workers" (Rom. 16:3). As we track them through the New Testament we see them always mentioned as a couple. But the order of their names varies, implying that they were equals in ministry.

Aquila and Priscilla established a home in Ephesus. After Paul left them there, he continued on his missionary journey through Judea and Syria, to Antioch and then back to Ephesus (Acts 19:1). While Paul was away from Ephesus, Aquila and Pricilla established a church in their home. When Paul came back to Ephesus, he wrote the book of 1 Corinthians. At the end of that book, he sent Aquila and Priscilla's greetings and greetings from the church that met at their house (1 Cor. 16:19).

As Priscilla and Aquila were getting established in Ephesus, they attended the Jewish synagogue. Paul had preached about Jesus in this synagogue and received a warm welcome (1 Cor. 16:19–20). While they were at this synagogue, they met a Jewish man named Apollos.

WORDS FROM WESLEY
Acts 18:21

I must by all means keep the feast at Jerusalem—This was not from any apprehension, that he was obliged in conscience to keep the Jewish feasts; but to take the opportunity of meeting a great number of his countrymen to whom he might preach Christ, or whom he might further instruct, or free from the prejudices they had imbibed against him. *But I will return to you*—So he did, ch. 19:1. (ENNT)

Background of Apollos (Acts 18:24–25)

Apollos (v. 24) was from Alexandria, then the capital of Egypt. Alexandria was famous for its library, the largest in the world, housing over five hundred thousand books. This was an impressive collection considering that the printing press had yet to be invented. Therefore, Alexandria attracted scholars from all around the world and became a center of learning. It also became a center of Old Testament studies. Here the Hebrew Bible was translated into Greek. A strong and learned Jewish population resided in that city. Verse 24 says **Apollos . . . was a learned man**. He had spent time in the library and among scholars of his town. The verse also records that he knew the Old Testament well. He had probably spent time in the school for the Old Testament in Alexandria.

Somewhere in his journeys, Apollos had heard about Jesus. **He had been instructed in the way of the Lord** (v. 25). Somebody, somewhere, had explained the story of Jesus. They told the story accurately but incompletely. **He knew only the baptism of John** (v. 25). So, when Apollos spoke passionately about Jesus, he spoke accurately but incompletely. He would tell the story of Jesus and tell people their response to the person of Jesus must be repentance. He would tell them to be baptized to demonstrate their willingness to turn from their old ways of life. He did not understand the full message of the gospel.

Later, Paul would meet other disciples of Christ like Apollos (19:1–5). Paul would explain to them that there is more to the gospel than repentance. Repentance is only one side of the equation. We must then trust the work of Jesus to connect us to God. We must move into Jesus and allow Jesus through His Holy Spirit to move into us. That is the full gospel.

Pricilla and Aquila perceived that Apollos understood only the first part of the gospel.

WORDS FROM WESLEY
Acts 18:25

This man had been instructed—Though not perfectly, in the way of the Lord—In the doctrine of Christ. Knowing only the baptism of John—Only what John taught those whom he baptized, namely, To repent and believe in a Messiah shortly to appear. (ENNT)

Mentoring Apollos (Acts 18:26)

Aquila and Priscilla **invited** Apollos **to their home**. There they **explained . . . the way of God more adequately** (v. 26). What Aquila and Priscilla did for Apollos made an impact on the church (vv. 27–28).

Mentoring has an impact on the church. In any mentoring relationship, a mentor has to have something to give, and the person being mentored has to be able to receive. In this mentoring relationship, the people giving were simple tentmakers. The person receiving was a "learned man." Yet the simple tentmakers had spent time with Paul and through him knew Jesus. They had experienced the power of the Spirit of God in their lives. They knew what it meant to suffer for Christ. They knew what it meant to live life with Jesus at their core. That relationship with Christ is what qualified them to be mentors.

Apollos had a theological education. He was a scholar. He was articulate. He was a leader. He was bold in his proclamation of what he believed. If we judged by the standards of this world, Apollos should have mentored Aquila and Priscilla. But in the kingdom of God, what matters is the depth of a person's relationship with God.

If one is going to be mentored in a manner consistent with the kingdom of God, humility will be required. *Humility* is best defined as a known dependence on God. It took humility for Priscilla and Aquila to approach this educated theologian to talk theology with him. It took humility for Apollos to hear what they had to say, rather than depend on his own learning.

WORDS FROM WESLEY

Acts 18:26

He spake—Privately; and taught publicly. Probably he returned to live at Alexandria, soon after he had been baptized by John; and so had no opportunity of being fully acquainted with the doctrines of the Gospel, as delivered by Christ and his Apostles. *And explained to him the way of God more perfectly.*—He who knows Christ, is able to instruct even those that are mighty in the Scriptures. (ENNT)

Learning and Leaving (Acts 18:27–28)

Scripture does not say how long Apollos stayed in Ephesus. But verse 27 seems to indicate that he integrated into the church at Ephesus and made himself accountable to the Christians there. He talked over his ministry plan with the believers of Ephesus and sought their confirmation. The text does not record anything about the impact Apollos made on the Ephesian church. But it does tell us he made a significant impact in the church in **Achaia** (v. 27).

Apollos needed the time in Ephesus to grow. He was moving from a Christianity that was something he did to something Christ did in him. He was moving from a kind of Christianity that was about repentance to the kind of Christianity that was about Christ being fully formed within him (Gal. 4:19). This kind of transition takes time. But this time prepared him for the service he was about to enter.

Aquila and Pricilla's mentoring did not discount Apollos' previous learning. When he went **to Achaia**, he helped those who believed and he debated from **the Scriptures** (Acts 18:27–28). That ability to debate and that scriptural learning had been formed before he met the ministry couple. But now his ministry was empowered by the Spirit of God.

In this section of Acts, we see the practical outworking of the body of Christ. Paul mentored Aquila and Priscilla. Some unknown person introduced Apollos to the life of Christ. Priscilla and Aquila mentored Apollos into the fullness of the life of Christ. The church at Ephesus gave Apollos a place to mature in faith. Apollos felt called to Achaia. This call was encouraged and facilitated by the Christians of Ephesus, who wrote a letter of introduction to the church in Achaia (v. 27).

The church in **Achaia** found Apollos to be **a great help to those who by grace had believed** (v. 27). Through Apollos, the church in Achaia was helped by Paul, by the unknown person who told Apollos about Jesus, by Aquila and Priscilla, and by the church in Ephesus. All these people influenced Apollos. So when he ministered, the ones who had invested in him were in a sense speaking as well.

If Paul hadn't invested in Priscilla and Aquila, or if Aquila and Priscilla hadn't invested in Apollos, the church in Achaia would have been impoverished. The work of the Spirit would have been hindered. It is possible we would have been impoverished as well.

WORDS FROM WESLEY

Acts 18:27

Who greatly helped through grace—It is through grace only that any gift of any one is profitable to another. *Them that had believed*—Apollos did not plant, but water. This was the peculiar gift which he had received. And he was better able to convince the Jews, than to convert the heathens. (ENNT)

This web of relationships that comprised the experience of Apollos became the dwelling place of God. People investing in people is the way the body of Christ was meant to function. Sometimes these are long-term relationships. Other times these relationships take place over a short period. But God builds us together and works through this bonding by His Spirit. We need each other.

DISCUSSION

In some school districts, knowledgeable students mentor lower-grade students or students who simply have a hard time learning. Knowledgeable believers are called to mentor others in God's Word.

1. Read Acts 18:1–4. How did God turn an apparently bad situation into a good one?

2. Why do you agree or disagree that Christian hospitality is declining?

3. Why do you agree or disagree that pastors should not engage in bivocational secular work? What negatives and/or positives do you associate with a pastor's secular employment?

4. Read 1 Corinthians 16:19. What further evidence do you find that Pricilla and Aquila were hospitable?

5. Do you think your church would benefit if members opened their homes more often for fellowship? If so, how would it benefit?

6. Aquila and Priscilla moved often throughout the Roman Empire. What advice would you give a Christian couple who had to move to a distant city?

7. Why did Apollos need to be mentored by Aquila and Priscilla?

8. Why do other Christians need you? Why do you need them?

PRAYER

Father, thank You for those who paved the way for our faith in You. Thank You for those who have helped us grow. Help us to continually seek such people out and to be that kind of person for someone else.

FINISHING THE RACE

Acts 20:17–38

The Holy Spirit enables us to finish well.

Images of mangled runners injured by terrorist bombings in the 2013 Boston Marathon may remain in our memories for the rest of our lives. Some of the victims were so close to the finish line when the two blasts occurred, but they were unable to complete the race. The Boston Marathon will continue to draw runners from around the world and big crowds in spite of the bombings.

When the apostle Paul neared the end of his ministry, he described the character of his ministry and promised to persevere in spite of imminent threats. He challenged the elders to fulfill their ministry and guard themselves and their flock. This study will inspire you to keep on keeping on!

COMMENTARY

At the time of the events described in the verses for this study, Paul was heading back east from his third missionary journey. He had spent most of the time—about three years—in Ephesus. It was the longest time he spent establishing any church.

Paul had a successful but turbulent ministry in Ephesus. We are told "all the Jews and Greeks who lived in the province of Asia heard the word of the Lord" (Acts 19:10). Everyone in Ephesus and the surrounding area was reached—saturation evangelism in the first century. So many of the worshipers of Diana (or Artemis) were becoming Christians that the charm manufacturers' union felt threatened. They started a riot that brought the city into the open-air theater loudly protesting the threatened rejection of their goddess. Paul left the city shortly after that riot.

Paul went west to Macedonia and Achaia (modern-day Greece) to visit the Philippians and Corinthians and other churches. He was taking up a collection for the needy Christians in Judea. He then doubled back and took ship for the eastern Mediterranean. It was on this route that he sailed past Ephesus and stopped at Miletus, a city about thirty miles south of Ephesus on the coast of modern-day Turkey.

Finishing Well Reflects Faithful Service (Acts 20:17–21)

From Miletus, Paul sent to Ephesus for the elders of the church (v. 17). One might wonder why Paul had not stopped at Ephesus rather than going on to Miletus, then waiting three days for someone to go to Ephesus and bring the elders back to him. Paul may have known that a visit to the church at Ephesus would have involved a lot more than three days, as the people would have urged him to stay for awhile. He was in a hurry to reach Jerusalem by the day of Pentecost (20:16).

Elders of the churches were important to Paul. He and Barnabas had appointed elders at each church they established on their first missionary journey (14:23). He later mentioned elders in writing to Timothy (1 Tim. 4:14; 5:17–20) and instructed Titus about who should be appointed to such an office (Titus 1:5–9). A board of elders served as the leaders of each local church, and they were often preachers and teachers. They tended to be the more mature believers in age and/or length of Christian experience.

Paul's address to the elders is one of four of his messages recorded in Acts (see Acts 13:16–41; 14:14–17; 17:22–31). This is the only one to a totally Christian audience. He began by reminding them of how he had ministered to them in Ephesus. **"You know how I lived the whole time I was with you, from the first day I came into the province of Asia"** (20:18). He mentioned his **humility** and **tears** and being **severely tested by the plots of the Jews** (v. 19). There is no record in Acts 19 of Jewish opposition to Paul's ministry in Ephesus, only that of the Gentiles. But it is obvious from the reference here that such did occur.

WORDS FROM WESLEY

Acts 20:19

Serving—See the picture of a faithful servant! *The Lord*—Whose the church is, *with all humility, and with tears, and trials*—These are the concomitants of it. The service itself is described more particularly in the following verse. This humility he recommends to the Ephesians themselves, Eph. 4:2. His tears are mentioned again, ver. 31 as also 2 Cor. 2:4; Phil. 3:18. These passages laid together, supply us with the genuine character of St. Paul. Holy tears, from those who seldom weep on account of natural occurrences, are no mean specimen of the efficacy and proof of the truth of Christianity. Yet joy is well consistent therewith (v. 24). The same person may be *sorrowful, yet always rejoicing*. (ENNT)

He also reminded them he had preached a full gospel, not hesitating **to preach anything that would be helpful to** them. He had **taught . . . publicly and from house to house** (20:20). The latter was characteristic of the early church (5:42). Paul's message had been the same to both Jews and Greeks. Two things were primary in his preaching: **they must turn to God in repentance**, thus turning away from their old lives, **and have faith in our Lord Jesus** (20:21). Repentance brings abandonment of what has been, and faith brings the spiritual power for new life. They represent the core of the gospel message.

Paul had laid a solid foundation for finishing well in his ministry by the faithful way he started in Ephesus.

Finishing Well Requires Perseverance (Acts 20:22–24)

Paul turned from reminding the Ephesian elders of his ministry to them and the church they represented to talk about what was ahead of him. He firmly declared that he was **compelled by the Spirit** (v. 22). The book of Acts speaks often of how definite the Holy Spirit's leadership was in Paul's ministry. There was the encounter on the road to Damascus and the Lord's clear instructions to Paul as to his ministry to the Gentiles. He had been forbidden by the Spirit to enter Asia and Bithynia early on his second missionary journey (16:6–7). Shortly after that, a vision directed him to go to Macedonia, which he did (16:9–10). He not only had in mind to go to Jerusalem, but he had said shortly before leaving Ephesus, "I must visit Rome also" (19:21).

Paul was headed for Jerusalem. He admitted **not knowing what** would **happen to** him **there** (20:22). He did **know that in every city the Holy Spirit** was warning him **that prison and hardships** awaited him (v. 23). Later, when Paul arrived in Caesarea, a few miles from Jerusalem, a prophet named Agabus told him that the Jews in Jerusalem would bind him and hand him over to the Gentiles. Luke and others begged him not to go to Jerusalem (21:10–14). But Paul was saying at Miletus that the Holy Spirit had been alerting him to this all along.

Paul was not deterred by the threat of danger. He considered his **life worth nothing** to him (20:24). What he was concerned about was to **finish the race and complete the task the Lord Jesus** had **given** him — **the task of testifying to the gospel of God's grace** (v. 24). Beginning well was not enough. Finishing well was the only acceptable goal. It is exciting to read what he wrote near the end of his life: "I have fought the good fight, I have finished the race, I have kept the faith" (2 Tim. 4:7). Paul reached his goal. It is interesting to note that he was to testify to the gospel of God's grace. Paul emphasized that salvation in Christ is not earned, it is a gift God freely gives. He wrote to the church at Ephesus, "For it is by grace you have been saved, through faith—and this not from yourselves, it is the gift of God—not by works, so that no one can boast" (Eph. 2:8–9).

●

WORDS FROM WESLEY

Acts 20:24

Nor do I count my life precious—It adds great force to this and all the other passages of Scripture, in which the apostles express their contempt of the world, that they were not uttered by persons like Seneca and Antoninus, who talked elegantly of despising the world in the full affluence of all its enjoyments: but by men who daily underwent the greatest calamities, and exposed their lives in proof of their assertions. (ENNT)

Finishing Well Requires Passing on Responsibility (Acts 20:25–32)

Paul believed his ministry to the Ephesians had been completed and that none of these elders would ever see him again. It is possible he was wrong about this, as several years later he wrote to Timothy at Ephesus indicating his plan to visit him there (1 Tim. 1:3; 3:14; 4:13). But he sensed he must leave the ministry to these leaders.

He referred again to his past ministry. He declared that he was **innocent of the blood of all men** (Acts 20:26). He stressed that he had **not hesitated to proclaim . . . the whole will of God** (v. 27). Probably his claim of innocence harkens back to Ezekiel 3:17–19. The Lord had told the prophet that He was appointing him as "a watchman for the house of Israel." If the Lord chose to punish a person for sin and Ezekiel did not warn that person, the Lord would hold Ezekiel responsible for that individual's blood. Paul had recognized he was under the same solemn obligation.

Paul then gave specific instructions to the elders. They were to **keep watch over** themselves **and all the flock** (Acts 20:28).

Their responsibility began with maintaining their own relationship with the Lord and out of their own faithfulness to minister to the congregation. It is interesting that those called "elders" in verse 17 are called **overseers** (also translated "bishops") and **shepherds** (pastors) in verse 28. So, at this point in the church's history, these titles seem to have been interchangeable.

WORDS FROM WESLEY
Acts 20:28

Take heed therefore—I now devolve my care upon you; first *to yourselves*; then *to the flock over which the Holy Ghost hath made you overseers*—For no man, or number of men, upon earth, can constitute an *overseer*, bishop, or any other Christian minister. To do this, is the peculiar work of the Holy Ghost: *To feed the church of God*—That is, the believing, loving, holy children of God. *Which he hath purchased*—How precious is it then in His sight! *With his own blood*—For it is the blood of the only begotten Son of God, 1 John 1:7. (ENNT)

Paul continued the image of shepherds and flock by warning them about **savage wolves** that would **come** and **not spare the flock** (v. 29). Jesus had also warned His disciples about false prophets who were ferocious wolves in sheep's clothing (Matt. 7:15). The wolves were those who would divide, scatter, and devour the true believers. They were those who would teach false doctrines, contradict the truth. Paul went on to warn them that some of their **own number** would **arise and distort the truth** hoping **to draw away disciples after them** (Acts 20:30). So he pled with them to **be on . . . guard!** (v. 31). He referred again to his ministry in which **for three years** he had warned them **night and day with tears** (v. 31).

This message to the elders gives us an insight into Paul's personality that we might otherwise miss. He comes across as such a strong, brave, dynamic leader. But in verses 19 and 31 he twice mentioned the tears he had shed in Ephesus. There was a tender, emotional side to Paul.

Paul concluded passing on responsibility to these elders by committing them **to God and to the word of his grace** (v. 32). The **word of his grace** could refer to the gospel message or to the promises of God. This word could build them up. It could give them **an inheritance among all those who are sanctified** (v. 32). **Sanctified** here probably refers to the process of sanctification, beginning with setting the person apart from sin to God that occurs at conversion, and to the entire sanctification that occurs when God cleanses the heart from sin and the Holy Spirit fills the believer, culminating in glorification when the believer is admitted to God's eternal presence. Paul spoke later to the Ephesians about the Holy Spirit being "a deposit guaranteeing our inheritance until the redemption of those who are God's possession" (Eph. 1:14).

Finishing Well Requires Proper Priorities (Acts 20:33–38)

Paul then referred the elders to one of the principles he had followed in his ministry at Ephesus: **"I have not coveted anyone's silver or gold or clothing"** (v. 33). Paul mentioned this often enough in his letters that it seems likely his enemies accused him of being in it for what he got out of it (1 Cor. 9:12; 2 Cor. 2:17; 9:2; 11:9; 12:14–19). He reminded them they knew his hands had supplied his own needs and those of his companions. Paul was a tentmaker and supported himself by practicing his trade as he went from church plant to church plant. (See 1 Cor. 4:12; 1 Thess. 2:9; 2 Thess. 3:7–8.) Paul had demonstrated to them **that by this kind of hard work we must help the weak** (Acts 20:35). **The weak** probably referred to anyone who had needs, especially those dependent on others for life's necessities. Then he cited a quotation from Jesus that does not appear in any of the four gospels: **"It is more blessed to give than to receive"** (v. 35). While not given in this form in the Gospels, it is in accord with other statements of Jesus (Luke 6:38). Paul was saying that with him it was a priority to give, rather than for others to give to him. Such a priority will help Christ's followers to finish well.

Verses 36–38 contain one of the most tender scenes in the New Testament as Paul and the Ephesian elders bid each other good-bye. There was weeping, embracing, and kissing—the holy kiss mentioned several times in the New Testament. **What grieved them most was his statement that they would never see his face again** (v. 38).

WORDS FROM WESLEY

Acts 20:37

They all wept—Of old, men, yea, the best and bravest of men, were easily melted into tears; a thousand instances of which might be produced from profane as well as sacred writers. But now, notwithstanding the effeminacy which almost universally prevails, we leave those tears to women and children. (ENNT)

DISCUSSION

What would you say if you were asked to share your experiences at a farewell dinner hosted by your church in your honor? Paul delivered a farewell address to the elders of the church at Ephesus.

1. Read Acts 20:18–21. What do you appreciate most about the way Paul ministered at Ephesus? Why does that aspect of his ministry hold the greatest appeal for you?

2. Why do you agree or disagree that door-to-door evangelism would have limited success today?

3. What dangers might await missionaries in developing countries?

4. On a scale of zero to ten, how strongly do you think you will finish the Christian race well? How can you raise your number?

5. Why do you agree or disagree that, regardless of one's accomplishments, finishing the Christian race well is of the utmost importance?

6. Read Acts 20:28–31. How can a pastor maintain the spiritual health of God's flock?

7. What distortions of the truth are you aware of?

8. How will you follow the zealous and faithful example Paul set?

PRAYER

Father, thank You for the example of Paul, who demonstrated perseverance in faith despite opposition. Help us to never leave one task You assign to us undone, that we too might persevere and run the race with excellence.

WORDS FROM WESLEY WORKS CITED

ENNT: *Explanatory Notes upon the New Testament,* by John Wesley, M.A. Fourth American Edition. New York: J. Soule and T. Mason, for the Methodist Episcopal Church in the United States, 1818.

PW: *The Poetical Works of John and Charles Wesley.* Edited by D. D. G. Osborn. 13 vols. London: Wesleyan-Methodist Conference Office, 1868.

WJW: *The Works of John Wesley.* Third Edition, Complete and Unabridged. 14 vols. London: Wesleyan Methodist Book Room, 1872.

OTHER BOOKS IN THE
WESLEY BIBLE STUDIES SERIES

Now Available in the
Wesley Bible Studies Series

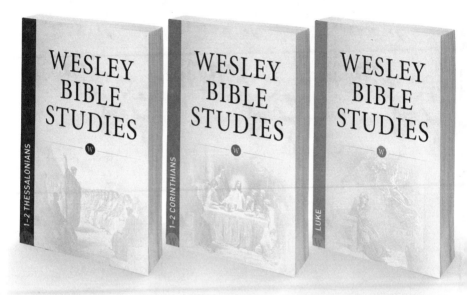

Each book in the Wesley Bible Studies series provides a thoughtful and powerful survey of key Scriptures in one or more biblical books. They combine accessible commentary from contemporary teachers, with relevantly highlighted direct quotes from the complete writings and life experiences of John Wesley, along with the poetry and hymns of his brother Charles. For each study, creative and engaging questions foster deeper fellowship and growth.

1–2 Thessalonians
978-0-89827-874-3
978-0-89827-875-0 (e-book)

Luke
978-0-89827-880-4
978-0-89827-881-1 (e-book)

1–2 Corinthians
978-0-89827-884-2
978-0-89827-885-9 (e-book)

1.800.493.7539 wphstore.com